Cellular
Business
Intelligence

PAULO ANDREOLI

Cellular Business Intelligence

A matter of survival

Foreword
Raquel Janissek-Muniz

English Version
Adolfo Carlos von Randow

© 2017 by Paulo Andreoli

Also published in Portuguese/Brazil with the title
Cellular Business Intelligence: uma questão de sobrevivência
by Paulo Andreoli Editor, São Paulo, 2017.

Editorial project
Eliana Sá

Cover and graphic design
Silvia Massaro

Proofreader
Margô Negro

Dados Internacionais de Catalogação na Publicação (CIP)
(Câmara Brasileira do Livro, SP, Brasil)

Andreoli, Paulo
  Cellular Business Intelligence : a matter of survival / Paulo Andreoli ; foreword Raquel Janissek-Muniz ; English version Adolfo Carlos von Randow. — São Paulo : Ed. do Autor, 2017.

  Bibliografia.
  ISBN: 978-85-923566-1-3

  1. Comunicação - Inovações tecnológicas 2. Comunicação nas organizações 3. Estratégia 4. Inteligência Antecipativa 5. Negócios 6. Sistemas de comunicação móvel 7. Tecnologia da informação e comunicação 8. Telefones celulares I. Janissek-Muniz, Raquel. II. Título.

17-08189   CDD-658.45

Índices para catálogo sistemático:
1. Comunicação corporativa : Administração 658.45

All the rights reserved to Paulo Andreoli Editor
paulo.andreoli@mslgroup.com
Published and printed in São Paulo, São Paulo, Brazil

SUPPORT:

This book is dedicated to the entrepreneurs,
the CEOs, the corporate communication
professionals and to my master
and source of inspiration, Maurice Levy

SUMMARY

FOREWORD — Raquel Janissek-Muniz	9
INTRODUCTION	11
Chapter 1 What are you afraid of?	23
Chapter 2 Inverting the signals	29
Chapter 3 Information: the main intangible asset of the XXI Century	35
Chapter 4 Just a man	51
Chapter 5 A simple, low-cost and intelligent structure	69
Chapter 6 The differential in Cellular Business Intelligence - CBI	81
Chapter 7 Personnel preparation, CBI's great challenge	95
CLOSING REMARKS And when your dog wags his tail...	111
ACKNOWLEDGEMENTS	119
CBI TEAM	121
ABOUT THE AUTHOR	125
BIBLIOGRAPHIC REFERENCES	127

FOREWORD

The word "intelligence" comes from the Latin language. It originates from "intelligere", comprising "intel", which means "between" and "legere", which means to know how to make a choice, to elect amongst several elements, to know how to read; the latter means to know how to put letters together. Therefore, intelligence is about knowing how to read between the lines, understanding, noticing, to notice and to know how to distinguish about certain issues. The verb to anticipate, in turn, has been borrowed from Latin, "antecipare", which comprises "ante" (before) and "capere" (to take); meaning to advance, to do (something) before it is expected.

When we associate the two elements, what we have is the Anticipative Intelligence concept, which means to have the ability to imagine, from information elements observed within the organizational environment, one or several potential outcomes. To anticipate is to defend a universe in which the future is not fate, it is not laid out, established and forecast, and is not part of a trend, but can be put together progressively, according to our acts and decisions. It is also the result of the sense (understanding) and of our interpretations of its possible consequences.

This book, *Cellular Business Intelligence*, is also the

result of a choice, of the ability to imagine and associate information elements observed throughout one's life by someone who is experienced in creating a future that can be achieved. This book is the product of the associative aspiration of a professional who has market experience, talent in his bloodstream, and knowledge of the backstage practices in the corporate world.

Paulo Andreoli, with his communication talent, has long been engaged with Anticipative Intelligence, in an intuitive way, by recognizing and anticipating the impact of the power and decision-making interconnections amongst agencies, departments, clients, stakeholders and large government and private-sector organizations.

By putting together all that he learned throughout his career with the intent to improve on what he had been doing as second nature, Mr. Andreoli has sought, in theory, elements that could provide the underpinnings to his understanding of the theme. In Anticipative Intelligence he found the theoretical foundation to back his ideas up. And that is how I got involved with the process.

Having studied Anticipative Intelligence during my doctoral studies, under the aegis of Professor Humbert Lesca – a living legend – at Université Pierre Mendès-France in Grenoble, I returned to Brazil with ambitious plans. As I got off the plane I had a challenge in mind: I wanted to share, in Brazil, the knowledge I had acquired throughout four unforgettable years as a member of a French research team (veille-strategique.org).

My plan was to put together initiatives that would encompass the academic and the corporate communities. As a matter of fact, I have always believed that the association between academia and business should be one of the main goals behind scientific research efforts. Thus, it was a challenge for me to put on record, academically speaking, the empirical evidence found in the dynamic flow between science and business practice, while I tried to articulate scientific research as a relevant factor, as something recognized as valuable for the business environment.

Bearing this challenge in mind, I returned to the School of Business Administration of Universidade Federal do Rio Grande do Sul (UFRGS), where I started my post-doctoral studies. Such studies would kickstart my activities in the following years. A lot has been achieved since then! Research, projects, publication, lectures, courses, consultancy work... In this context, the Anticipative Intelligence concept grew exponentially, having been given a slingshot by our academic initiatives, some inroads into professional environments, and also, of course, due to the evolution of the understanding, on the part of corporations, of the importance of monitoring the environment through formal and structured intelligence processes.

But science thrives on economic stimulus, and I felt the academia – corporation bridge had to be strengthened. In fact, all of our research efforts, even though they were supported by numerous studies, sought for something that could reinforce the interaction amongst these worlds. Then Mr. Andreoli asked to see me. We had a conversation that was a perfect fit for my desire to get these two worlds together.

I believe we find room whenever we are ready to find new roads. The roads intersected, the conversations flowed, and a team was put together. Different views of the same issues came up, the awareness grew stronger, and a solution was developed. The results are manifold: a complementary understanding; a new concept that puts together the best from academia and the best from the entrepreneurial world, a solution that is not limited into itself, but rather, one which acquires more value as perception and cooperation come along; a new intelligence gateway: *Cellular Business Intelligence* (CBI).

This book, which Mr. Andreoli went ahead and organized, has been devised for those who believe the world evolves and the ensuing changes are more than inevitable. In fact, they are desirable! They also bring uncertainties, but following this evolution by careful and selected monitoring of anticipating signals is one way of surging ahead and maintaining a business with sustainability and perpetuity. Teams that are aware of the strategic importance of staying ahead of the market seek to keep their vantage point by supporting themselves on established Anticipative Intelligence processes.

For those who seek to delve deeper into the concept and into the vast theoretical underpinnings of the solution, free access is provided to the academic gateway (ieabrasil.com.br). If you are amongst those who seek practical application, you can follow the roadmap that wraps this well-articulated book together, enabling CBI to count on the best from academia and the best from the corporate world as far as intelligence is concerned. Academia benefits from the practical application of our research's concepts. Corporations benefit from a unique and innovative Anticipative Intelligence approach. We all benefit from the endless loop and from continuous reinforcement provided by the scientific-economic stimulae. I am honored to participate in this project.

Dr. Raquel Janissek-Muniz

INTRODUCTION

As a journalist and communicator, I always planned to write a book. To tell the truth, the first step would be to conclude a collection of short stories that I have been working on for over ten years. The stories tell bits and pieces of my life as seen by an old man called Natali, a character I created to honor a former fellow journalist who always urged me to create something, tapping away at the keyboard.

But it looks like Mr. Natali will have to wait a little longer to show his philosophy to the readers. According to my original plans, I should finish that first inroad into fiction in a small house on a mountaintop, after I leave the stress aful executive and entrepreneur routine behind.

Therefore, this book that you, dear reader, now have before your eyes, had not been a part of my plan. What prompted me to write it was a professional challenge that took place at a pivotal moment of my life as a corporate communication executive. Looking into the future, that one pieces together in the present, by relating and integrating issues that I evaluate in my agency and with my clients, a question overshadowed all fiction:

What is the future of public relations, corporate communications or corporate affairs agencies? What sort of outlook can we piece together to integrate such agencies into a world that has been changed by the digital revolution?

I hope this book provides the answers to these questions. I will begin it by telling my own story.

I established my first agency 23 years ago in a small, borrowed office, in Brooklin, a neighborhood in the South side of São Paulo. The office was not actually the agency, since I had not figured I would have one. I would say it was a place for me to stay. I would leave my house early in the morning and would go to that small office. Once there, I would sit at the desk, and from there, using a telephone, which, by the way, was also borrowed, I would keep in touch with my leads, seeking opportunities.

Less than a month later I realized that my earnings surpassed the salary I had been paid as the head of corporate affairs for one of the leading communication groups in Brazil, and probably also surpassed the earnings I would have achieved had I accepted the job that had been offered to me as an executive of a corporate group in the interior of the São Paulo state.

One must keep in mind that back then, in the early 1990s, we lived in a different world: there were no cellphones and the internet was still around the corner. We worked with limited resources. But when I established the agency I already envisioned communication as a part of a larger strategy in the business plan. And this was the beginning of Paulo Andreoli Corporate Affairs, which intended to use communication as a tool geared towards serving companies' strategic interests. When we say communication, we mean the company's relations with its various target audiences and various media, working at the core of the company, and not only as resource to be employed occasionally, such as events, products releases, conferences and other activities spread out throughout the fiscal year.

That was trail-blazing work around 1993, and, possibly, this view of the market was the reason for the overnight success of that small agency that was growing, and that provided good earnings for me, as well as profits for my clients. In this respect, the relationships I had forged with entrepreneurs and CEOs of large corporations throughout my press career were certainly key elements for what one could call success.

Outgoing as a reporter, brazen like an entrepreneur, and most likely, arrogant like a desperate person, I elbowed my way in, re-establishing contacts and marketing my services.

The people who agreed to see me, either out of sympathy or politeness, would generally schedule a meeting at the end of the day, a time which busy and polite people offer as a quota to unexpected visitors. Relaxed after a stressful day, executives would describe their problems, fears and expectations. Based on that frank and honest disclosure, I would return a few days later, bringing solutions or ideas that could be useful to dispel their concerns. Thus, without making much of an effort, and putting my expertise to work, I would sell what was an obvious thing to me. But that was an obvious thing that was unconcerned with the inner workings of corporate policy, unconcerned with the fear of making a mistake; it was an obvious thing from "an outsider", with no preconceptions, blunt, and without a spark of magic.

I would be honest to say that oftentimes the solutions for the corporate problems were to be found within the company itself, hiding in corporate silos, and protected from view by trenches filled with people who held information, possibly hidden even by higher management.

Let's face it, the corporate environment is not the best environment for the free flow of information, even the potentially strategic information. Corporations, even the large ones, at some point in time, function like local neighborhoods within small towns in the countryside: meetings are held within small corporate ghettos, people live from day to day by the force of gossip, they peek through the window to see the color of the new car in the garage next door. They do not value whoever is working on the other cubicle or the department next door. There is a continuous struggle for survival which may oftentimes obliterate others. For many people who live in this small enclosed world, competition is to be found amongst the ranks of the company itself.

It is understandable that many corporations invest millions in order to establish the highest-quality in-house environments, probably under the assumption that it is possible to encourage sharing amongst departments, for the common good. I am sure many large corporations have achieved significant results, even though I know very few cases. I would rather stick to the general guidelines used by Maurice Levy, for whom the rules are simple: "No silo, no solo, no Bozo". In other words: no silos or groups; no single-handed work, no solitary geniuses, and no clowns.

Yes, there are clowns out there. And they are not to be found necessarily within circuses, which are few and far between these days. They may also be hiding within large corporations. And before you know it, they materialize unexpectedly to cause trouble. I could come up with a number of examples of the time during which there were no social networks in order to disclose their blunders within seconds. There was that case with in international airline captain who, upon deplaning at a Brazilian airport, was absent-mindedly approached by the local authorities. Irked, he showed his middle finger to the law-enforcement agent, unaware of the fact that he was having his picture taken. Next day the incident was front-page news on all main newspapers. This became an image crisis case. Just an employee in a bad mood.

How many such clowns do you know?

I cannot help but think of the communication teams trying to repair the reputation damage caused by these people. Recently, an executive well-known to me was unhappy due to the fact that he had lost a client. He blamed such loss on a competitor. He then posted an article on the internet. The article was in the format of a complaint. In the text, he compared his competitor, the founder or a leading communication group, to a brothel owner, and worse than that, he compared that group's upper management team to a bunch of prostitutes!

Any communication professional, used to the so-called reputation crises, could think of hundreds of similar stories.

As one can plainly see, that CEO that we visit at the end of the business day has a lot to complain about. In addition, think about this: how would he react if he became aware that important strategic data for his business is being thrown in the wastepaper basket downstairs from his office? I am sure he would be even more frustrated. How can we help him? How could I help integrate, to a larger extent, the tsunami of data that circulates through the company and finds its way to his desk through countless channels? How can we put our communication skills to work so as to benefit the business core?

My challenge within the last few years has been thinking over this possibility and pressing ahead with these ideas. The final push was triggered by a provocation. It came about during a meeting that I attended abroad.

A group of about 300 professionals, selected out of

a total of 70,000, was asked to share its views during a meeting held in the San Francisco area, in California, in September 2016. We had the opportunity to listen, in the legendary Silicon Valley, startup backers, entrepreneurs, innovators and visionaries. For example, we heard that, as of 2007, with the iPhone release, we plunged, at breakneck speed, into mankind's largest technological revolution. We attended an exhibit according to which if we multiply, by 30, all the knowledge that the iPhone has brought us and the changes resulting from it, that have had an accumulated effect on our lives, we can envision what is ahead of us within the next five years.

Are you ready? And, by the way, what does it mean to be ready?

It is obvious that when we first saw the iPhone we were surprised with its new features. All were able to experience, for the first time, the various applications, the touch screen that would increase the screen size with just the fingers' touch, and other innovations that made our jaws drop.

We could also say that many could envision other uses that would come about as a result of that device's technology. But who could imagine that an app would drastically change the way in which the music industry was organized? And what about the hospitality industry? Who could suppose that just one application would trigger the urban mobility Apps revolution, that, in spite of the cabdrivers' resistance, ended up disrupting the time-honored relationships between users and the means through which people move about the big cities?

Today's challenge could be termed as "our having had" the ability to foresee, back in 2007, something like Uber or iFood.

This was when I realized that, today's executives'

challenge is that they have to get ready for the new Apps that are just around the corner and anticipate their reactions with regard to what lies ahead. Impossible? Maybe. But the first step is, we must come to terms with the fact that, possibly, strategic planning is being carried out by looking at the rear view mirror, by looking at data we are aware of, and projecting such data into the near future. We have to realize that it is hard to plan so as to foresee the next turns, when the roadmap is not ready yet.

Maybe one can foresee the future based on information that is already available now, even through we cannot pinpoint it or redesign it within a new scenario in which it can go on projecting itself and taking on a new meaning?

This was the background for my musings on how communication agencies could provide their contribution in this complex state of affairs – in which a tremendous amount of data comes in every second and swiftly makes its way through corporations, urging me to think of ways to select, screen, evaluate, and interpret such data, and extract from it something that may enable us to foresee what "lies ahead".

Armed with a disposition to dig into these ideas, I put together a task force in my company and sought, within the academic community, both in Brazil and elsewhere, individuals engaged in the study of these issues, and the results of their intellectual efforts.

I painstakingly went over the work of a task force led by Professor Humberto Lesca, of Pierre Mendès-France University, Grenoble, France. It showed the same outlook of attempting to foresee the future based on weak signals identification, reading, interpretation and monitoring. In addition, the model created by the Professor Lesca values information sharing and the quest for "missing parts" in a strategic board, like the pieces of a jigsaw puzzle. It had a lot in common with the model we had been developing in São Paulo, although there were a few differences.

We had an even greater surprise when we found out that Raquel Janissek-Muniz, Universidade Federal do Rio Grande do Sul (UFRGS) professor, was amongst the PhD's that had created the weak signals theory in the same Grenoble task force. In the following week, Professor Raquel became a member of our team at Publicis Consultants, a strategic consultancy working under the aegis of MSLGROUP, the corporate communication branch of Publicis Group, which we are a part of.

I believe in synchronicity. Only a great coincidence could bring consultant Vitor Madeira to our team. He had just recently left the vice-president's seat at Accenture. This experienced and brilliant mind soon became a member of our theoretical study team.

Thus, supported by the team led by Claudia Mancini, head of Publicis Consultants in Brazil, Béatrice Seguin, Claudia's team, Raquel, Vitor and I, we had the task force that would delve deep into the issue, after hearing many CEOs of large companies talk about the strategic issues that concerned them, and about how anxious each one is to foresee the future in order to have a better foundation for the strategic decisions they have to make in the present.

This research core originated the *Cellular Business Intelligence*-CBI method concept, which shall be described at length in this book.

This method has a few underlying propositions, as follows:

• information that may enable one to read and foreseen the future;

- information with strategic responses to current and future challenges may be floating around in the room next door;
- strategic information may be flowing in fits and starts within the company, and may be lost since it is not shared amongst departments which seem to be watertight;
- information provides yields, and being power-hungry, many people end up withholding information, thus stanching a flow that is the company's lifeblood;
- and finally, even strategic information must be dealt with according to law-abiding and ethical practices.

Generally, we can disclose the fact that this method calls for the introduction of a CBI cell into the company, with a communication agency consultant and a company's coordinator, who will collect data and put together a panel, based on the weak signals theory, thus creating a kind of "time capsule" for the future. This capsule will show directions and hazards, enabling management to make decisions that will protect, in the present, the future of their organizations.

We want to help managers, especially CEO's, to introduce, in an organized, systematic manner, into the corporate culture, the practice whereby Anticipative Information is sought and analyzed, so as to enable the organization to define strategies, restore its image in the market, detect actions of opportunity and prevent crises.

We also sustain that a communication agency must be in charge of coordinating the CBI cell in the company. This is because we know that communication professionals are second to none in the business of dealing with information. Such professionals are used to dealing with the so-called sensitive corporate information. They are used to establishing the parameters for the use and disclosure of relevant, strategic and confidential information.

Thus, if a given company's CBI is able to identify, by looking at the information, weak signals that may compromise the business, the CBI will know **who** it must influence, **how** to influence, and **which language** it must use in order to do that.

Throughout the pages of this book, we will seek to explain our ideas and to clarify the roadmap for the Cellular Business Intelligence concept, always engaged in setting courses that may ensure a safer and smoother tomorrow.

Shall we make our way together?

CHAPTER 1

WHAT ARE YOU AFRAID OF?

> "During the latest global meeting promoted by hipster Singularity University, in California(...), the idea was to bring the future into the present. Thus, one comes to the conclusion that, rather than thinking about ROI (return on investment), one should think about COI, the cost of ignoring (changes, the future) – this can be lethal."
>
> NIZAN GUANAES
> *Folha de S. Paulo, August 29, 2017*

The Fobo concept – Fear of Becoming Obsolete – first appeared in Davos, Switzerland, during the World Economic Forum in January 2016. In this situation, the individual becomes so anxious due to the pace at which the world changes that he fears his career and his company may be left behind. The phenomenon was found by means of the worldwide Innovation Barometer survey, carried out by the U.S. General Electric Co.

The survey has been carried out for the fifth year in a row. 2,748 CEO's from 23 countries, including Brazil, in addition to 1,346 opinion makers, from 13 countries, were interviewed. Based on these two target audiences, the survey sought to find out how the perception of innovation was changing in a complex and globalized world. Executives and opinion makers agree that they must go through a radical makeover in order to keep abreast of what is going on.

In the survey, 90% of the respondents say that the most innovative companies not only roll out new products and services, but they also create markets that did not exist before. Nevertheless, they fear that technology is evolving at a quicker pace than they can keep up with. Amongst the world's executives, 81% were aware of the "digital darwinism", or the fear of becoming obsolete. And Brazilians – surprise! –

were leading that worldwide ranking: 90% of them feared the possibility of being swallowed by technology.

Today's vulnerabilities are very different from those that could be foreseen a few years back. I truly believe that what in fact bothers people is the perception that the technological innovation tsunami in fact exists and it is rushing towards the shore faster than we can run. What triggers this phobia is the fact that we are not sure which way we should run.

There is only one thing we are certain of: we can't just stand there. Should we run and choose the way to seek new talents who focus, to a larger extent, on the digital solutions? Should we follow the road that will enable us to re-structure our business? Or should we replace our core business altogether?

There are many paths for us to choose from. Survival will depend on whether you pick a route about which, at least, you have some information. It will be even better if, in addition to the information, you manage to foresee the risks inherent to this path – the steepest downhill slopes, the most dangerous curves, possible obstacles and geographical features that we can work our way around.

Remember, you must have something like Waze, a radar-like device that, in addition to pointing the strategic routes, will talk you through the shortest and safest path, that can show you where the roadblocks are, where the filling stations are (you may need them), where the restrooms are, as well as the resources to minimize or prevent any embarrassing situation and... moreover, that may ensure your survival.

Yes, this book is about survival.

Suppose you are an absent-minded person. Tonight you board a plane to Sweden, leaving from São Paulo. It is a summer day and you are wearing a polo shirt. In the morning you wake up in Stockholm. You forget to pick up your winter coat that is on your seat. The flight attendant opens the aircraft's door. The cold wind surprises you. And a voice inside your head says: if you get out of the plane like this you're dead. Then you walk back to your seat. You pick up your overcoat and put it on; you find a scarf in the overcoat's pocket, you wrap all that wool around your neck and yet your whole body shrinks.

The voice that gave you a heads-up about the cold is the voice of the "intelligent cells". These cells are the ones that cause an inflammation to quickly appear in your finger when it is inadvertently cut, even if the cut is a superficial one, while you are peeling an apple. These are the cells that heal your finger and put it back in shape, and ensure the survival of your body, by protecting it from outside threats.

I found these cells while I was doing some research on intelligence. I know that biology is not taught at business schools. Nevertheless, many management studies show the analogy between the way the human body works and the way companies are run.

At the present juncture, the viral threat is as harmful to human health as it is to corporate health. If, on one side, globalization facilitates the contamination of communities by new, sophisticated and different viruses, the social networks disseminate viral information at a pace that has the potential to destroy one's reputation or discredit corporate strategies in a matter of seconds.

Do companies currently need biologists in their board of directors? Not necessarily. But knowing how intelligent cells work may be a useful skill for corporate management in today's environment, since, both for the scientific community and for the executive board information is the only way to go if one wants quick and effective responses to prevent outside threats.

See the description of intelligent cells provided by

Professor Bruce H. Lipton, a cell biologist, 2009 Nobel Prize winner and author of the best-selling book *The Biology of Belief*:

"Cells analyze thousands of stimuli they receive from the environment they live in, in order to select the most appropriate responses and ensure their survival. Evolution's requirement so that cell communities were established is only the result of the biological need for survival. The better awareness an organism has with regard to the environment around it, the higher are its odds to survive. When cells get together, they exponentially increase their situational awareness.

These sophisticated communities subdivide their workload in a more precise and effective manner than our largest companies and world-class corporations. In larger organisms, only a percentage of the cells is responsible for reading and responding to the environmental stimuli. This role is played by groups of specialized cells that comprise the nervous system's tissues and organs. The nervous system's job is to acquire the environment's data and coordinate the behavior of all other cells in its large community."

Does it make any sense to imagine intelligent cells in your company in order to prevent outside threats and thus ensure your company's survival?

But what is the sense in intelligent cells and how could they ensure the company's survival?

My assumption is that the work of intelligent cells within companies, which would analyze information on certain strategic issues in the internal and external environments, would make it possible to create Anticipative Intelligence. Have I caused lights in your brain to illuminate? Let us go on. Some examples mentioned in the next few chapters may help explain how this works.

CHAPTER 2
INVERTING THE SIGNALS

> *"When social structures and behavior patterns become so rigid that society can no longer adapt to changing situations, it is incapable of pressing on with the creative process of cultural evolution."*
>
> FRITJOF CAPRA
> *The Turning Point*

Weak signals, a household concept for those who deal with Anticipative Intelligence, were specified as such by Igor Ansoff in the mid-nineteen seventies. Ansoff, a Russian-born American professor and consultant, graduated from Brown University with degrees in Engineering and Mathematics, and worked at RAND Corporation and Lockheed. He is known as the creator of strategic management. According to Ansoff, who introduced this concept in the business world, weak signals may be gleaned from a piece of information, intuition, a conversation, a testimonial, a document, a hint, or simply a talk between two executives seating ahead of you, aboard an airplane.

When identified and monitored, they may cease being just signals and may become a trend, which is not only perceptible but also feasible. There is a moment on which the weak signal is no longer weak. It becomes an assumption. This is the decision-making point: you either try to reverse the trend – acting upon the influencers that push it ahead – or you seek to adapt to what is coming.

The competitive difference of those who can, with information and intelligence, establish the "mutation point" (we are using a quantum physics term here) shall inevitably imply a competitive difference as compared to those who have no clue what is going on. The latter will only become aware that the fax machine is obsolete when somebody tells them that they will send all documents as e-mail attachments.

Take a break. Think and answer my question: You have been operating a fleet of taxis in town for a few years now. You practically control this market and you profit from it. But tell me: when did you first notice that black cars, with courteous drivers, who hand out water and candy, were "stealing" your clients?

Suppose you had a network of movie rental places. When did you notice that your neighbors would rather stay home, sitting on the sofa, watching Netflix movies?

You could also own an electronics store downtown. When did you notice that 23-year-old boy, your neighbor, was selling more stuff than you did, while working from his home, through a website established just a few months ago?

You are a shareholder of a large corporation that produces millions of automotive fire extinguishers. Your company has been selling parts to large car manufacturers. You have already put together millions of pieces for next year. And suddenly, the regulatory agency decides that your product is no longer of mandatory use in cars. Your sales experience a precipitous drop...

Without a doubt, there was a time when that regulatory agency's decision was nothing but a weak signal. It was certainly a signal that reached your company and was the subject of conversations for months at offices near your own, that circulated freely around the departments, through the factory floor. Your government relations and public affairs manager heard about this almost a year ago. He took pains to review this information and to keep it under wraps, since, after all, this possible decision could simply derail the business. Did he decide to wait? Did your sales manager also hear about this? What did he do about it? Your purchasing department intern's brother-in-law's cousin talked about it, among friends, at a bar. He said he read about this on Facebook, that a university in Southern Australia had carried out a scientific survey showing that a significant percentage of drivers would just forget they had a fire extinguisher when they had accidents. And that, due to that conclusion, they considered fire extinguishers just decorative accessories. Was this a weak signal?

Maybe now it is easier to understand the "fear of becoming obsolete". What can we say about large corporations, with tens of thousands of employees, hundreds of plants and offices spread around the world, dependent on certain products? Only innovation will save them? Yes, but that depends on the time they will have to react. The sooner they identify the weak signals and the more accurate the "mutation point" is, the easier they will survive the outside environment. That is, if the intelligence cells are able to tell, in due time, that the flight attendant opened the aircraft's door and the outside temperature is 15 degrees Celsius below zero.

As I review the previous paragraphs, I start to understand the agony of those whose job is to decide on the future of large corporations, of a medium-sized company, or even a small business. I see them all rowing their boats on a transparent blue water river with beautiful, leafy trees on the margins. All CEOs have a team of athletes. They are all in line, rowing a boat. I see that the boat goes steadily towards the future, which is on the bottom, still covered in a thick early morning fog. The curious thing about it is that even though they see that the teams are steady and sure of themselves, and even though they see how strongly and determined they row towards the future, they are all looking back, they have their backs to what lies ahead of them.

And would you be able to tell why they all feel so safe? It is because they are rowing based on what they think they know about where the river is taking them. But, wait, one of the teams stopped at the margin and started walking, having become the butt of jokes, being laughed at by those who would pass along, swift and smiling. Somebody had provided some interesting information, at breakfast time, to the team that was carrying the boat over their shoulders, before the start of the race: the fog is, actually the mist formed by the spray of a powerful waterfall...

The end of the rowing teams' story is trivial, since many of them are safe. They are all well. All of them are sucessful entrepreneurs now – but they are no longer taking part in a rowboat race. These days they are selling popcorn.

Yes, this may be the end of the story: either we are prepared to read the signs of change or we will just stop being competitive. There is nothing wrong with selling popcorn. Quite the opposite. This activity certainly will not put too many demands on our ability to foresee the future.

CHAPTER 3

INFORMATION: THE MAIN INTANGIBLE ASSET OF THE XXI CENTURY

> "Anticipative Information would be of interest, primarily to the would-be 20% of the issues left aside by the foreseers. It is in these issues that we could potentially find signs of possible rupture and innovation, and this would be of interest to an attentive organization."
>
> RAQUEL JANISSEK-MUNIZ

A little over 200 years ago, on June 18, 1815, in the Belgian fields, the Battle of Waterloo was fought. The battle was pivotal to the fate of Europe over the following decades. To this day, historians discuss the reasons that made Napoleon, who a hundred days before had escaped exile in the Isle of Elba, suffer such tremendous defeat in the hands of the British forces.

One of the generally accepted explanations is that the French emperor's troops were held back by a vicious storm. This delayed the attack on the British positions defended by the Duke of Wellington. Thus, the British were able to beat the French offensive back until the arrival of the Prussian troops led by Marshal von Blücher. That defeated Napoleon's strategy, since it had been his intent to fight one army at a time. The might of the British and Prussian forces put together defeated the French.

Whatever explanation applies to the episode, one thing is certain: the battle was not only pivotal to the future of Europe: it was also responsible for a notorious growth in the wealth of Baron Nathan Rothschild, the main character of an operation in the London Stock Exchange that went down in history. This took place because the baron obtained, before anyone else – and was able to use! – information about the British-Prussian victory in Waterloo. Thus, he sold, at the top of the market, with a good profit margin, that country's treasure bonds, which he had acquired a short time earlier, at rock-bottom prices. Other adventurous investors followed suit.

The versions on how Rothschild and other investors were able to have early access to this information – when the telegraph did not even exist – are as varied as the explanations for Napoleon's defeat. Rumor has it that an observer had been sent to the battlefield and that, as soon as he became aware of the outcome, he traveled on horseback, at breakneck speed, towards a port in the North of France, and then sailed to London. The trip by sea had been previously arranged. According to other reports, carrier pigeons were employed.

Historical research carried out recently indicates that neither version is correct. News of the British-Prussian victory was already known in London on June 21. The news was published by three of the dozens of one- or two-page newspapers that were sold in the city back then. The baron, therefore, read the news or became aware of the rumors and decided to use such information in his strategy to leverage his business at the Stock Exchange.

More than explanations and versions, what matters here is the ability to obtain, analyze and employ, in business management and corporate strategy, information that anticipates facts that disrupt or cause great changes in trends forecast for the environment outside the company. In today's parlance, such facts may be considered as small weak signals, indications or outliers. Specialists and researchers call these facts Anticipative Information.

Anticipative Information, mainly, originates outside the company, and is about the socioeconomic environment the company is part of, usually pointing at change, innovation and evolution. Such information is informal, incomplete, somewhat repetitive, uncertain, ambiguous, fragmented and contradictory. Nevertheless, when integrated to other information of the same kind and subjected to analysis, it enables the user to "create a different and innovative vision of the business opportunities that may present themselves as well as of the risks, that would not be so evident if we did not have this device", according to the study *Inteligência Estratégica Antecipativa e Coletiva para Tomada de Decisão*, [Anticipative, Collective and Strategic Intelligence for Decision-Making], signed by Raquel Janissek-Muniz, Humbert Lesca and Henrique Freitas.

For centuries, in peace or at wartime, in politics and in the business world, detecting and analyzing what may happen in the future, based on what is going on now, tend to ensure great advantages, yield significant profit, and, of course, anticipate loss or crisis situations. Research carried out by Strategic Intelligence experts even detected the relationship between obtaining and analyzing Anticipative Information and the competitiveness and sustainability of an organization.

We insist on using the terms "analysis" and "analyzing" to stress that Anticipative Information, in and of itself, does not mean a relevant difference for any organization. "If information pointed at anything, it would point at everyone who would be paying attention to it" says Humbert Lesca and Raquel Janissek-Muniz in their book.

In the same publication, the authors advise that organizations discard information that can be of great use if properly analyzed: "The Anticipative Information model would be interested, primarily, in what we would consider 20% of the data left aside by forecasters. It is in these issues that one could, potentially, find signs of possible rupture and innovation. That would certainly be of interest for the organization".

We see, then, that what makes the difference is the INTELLIGENCE applied in one's interpretation. But how do we get there?

Upon returning from her doctorate in France in 2004, Raquel Janissek-Muniz introduced, in Brazil, the concept of Anticipative, Collective and Strategic Intelligence [Inteligência Estratégica Anecipativa e Coletiva], IEAc, and the L.E.SCAnning method, created by the same study group she was a member of, at the University of Grenoble. In summary, this concept comprises a monitoring system, structured within the company, with specific methods for the collection, selection and interpretation of the anticipative data, especially weak signals.

Weak signals of value to the organization are especially difficult to distinguish from the social networks deluge. Usually they represent snippets, instead of strings of data that may help companies verify what their clients wish, and locate new segments or changes in the market – before the competition can do it.

One must have a specific method in order to be able to identify such data or information. But, before that, one must pay attention to the nature of information that the company has or that it may collect.

Summarizing, there are three groups of data that are of direct interest to the company, according to scholars Humbert Lesca and Raquel Janissek-Muniz:

These are:

1. **Operational information**: data existing within the company, that is indispensable for its operation. These data is operational, repetitive and formalized. For example: work orders; payroll; invoices; budget.

2. **Influential information:** may be issued in the internal or external environment, but has a direct impact on the team's behavior. For example: meetings, advertising, informal comments amongst professionals, planning, and scenarios.

3. **Anticipative Information:** defined previously.

A comparison amongst these kinds of information shall result in the following table, originating from the same study.

Operational information	Influential information	Anticipative Information
Existing within the organization	Existing both inside and outside the organization	Existing within the organization's business environment
Internal -> internal flow	Internal <-> external flow	External -> internal flow
Retrospective (rearview mirror)	Present (current time)	Prospective (headlights, radar)
Client's order, inventory record, pay stub, entry-exit control record, invoice, etc.	Meetings, ads, service notes, noise in the halls, products catalogs, etc.	Registration for a new product, Request to fill a new position, construction of a new plant, etc.

Therefore, operational information is essential for the organization's survival, since it records its history (past) and enables one to perform day-to-day management (present). But it is not strategic, since it does not point to the future.

The items that appear in the second group may or may not be considered strategic, depending on the way they are employed. For example, a scenario study or trends forecast.

Anticipative Information, in turn, is clearly strategic, to the extent that its goal is only to support management's decision-making. It may enable the organization to see possibilities that would hardly be noticed if the time-honored Strategic Intelligence instruments were to be employed, since it is the outlier.

The two examples below, in completely different economic sectors, show the difference and the utilization possibilities between influential and Anticipative Information. One case took place in the late 1990s, in Brazil, while state-run electric utilities were being privatized. It shows how the weak signal can work as a headlight for a company in a competition scenario.

The other took place in the soccer environment and shows the importance of market intelligence and trend indications.

In the late 1990s, a corporate group (I cannot mention its name for obvious reasons) put together, in-house, a team of professionals whose job was to structure the strategy for participating in the privatization auction of an electric power distribution utility. The latter was the object of desire of a number of local and foreign investors.

Evidently, as is the case in any dispute, the strategy, involving the bid to be submitted, would depend on detecting the profile of the other bidders – that was information that the official means, or the news disclosed by the press, would not provide in a satisfactory way. Besides, these investors could join the bidding process just moments before the dispute.

After outlining the profile of the competitors who stood out in the local market – using influential data – this group found a creative solution to detect outliers, or weak signals, that would indicate future trends, in case a competitor would join the bidding process just before the auction. On the eve of the event, the company sent employees to stay at five-star hotels located near the venue where the auction would take place. These employees had a single mission: to detect the language spoken by the hotels' guests. In other words, they had to find weak signals.

Once they had the answer, identifying the language spoken by the competitors, even without having access to the concept, they applied IEAc to the information and were able to ascertain whether the list of bidders would show any surprise that would represent a rupture in the trend outlined.

In the soccer environment, there are also many examples of the use of influential information before hiring players in order to put together a competitive group, collected by well-organized teams. European teams that enjoy continuous success have a regimented analysis system, as well as a vast database in order to analyze the performance of the players they intend to hire.

In Brazil, a soccer team started putting its database together in 2015. Even though it did not formally establish a system to collect weak signals, members of its management are keeping tabs on data that show ruptures or a re-directing of the trends for this database. This regimented follow-up comprises what is known as Strategic Information or Market Intelligence.

These are some of the data collected:

- Average of successful goals, assistance, passes, finalization, dribbling, as well as other requirements as compared with the average data for other players in the same position;
- Data on the player's physical and technical fitness; this can be ascertained, in the first case, through field research, by means of direct conversations with medical department professionals; in the second case, by means

of conversations with coaches and assistant coaches associated with the player;
• Psychological profile: with the aid of professionals in the area, one defines a psychological profile for the team; then one only hires and maintains players who are in compliance with that profile;
• History and path: a thorough analysis of the player's history and path through each team, in order to find details about his personality and technical ability;
• Age: player's performance analysis as compared with that of players in the same age group, in order to measure his potential, maturity and longevity.

It is important to observe how, with the passage of time, the evolution of the treatment given to the information of interest to the company has kept abreast of the progress of the means of communication.

Up until halfway through the XIX Century, companies and entrepreneurs had the luxury of being intuitive in this quest for Anticipative Information. When not even the telegraph was available, correspondence, written on paper, was handed to a courier who traveled on horseback, and the markets were basically local – the number of participants were much smaller than today's. That is, the amount of information was smaller, and it circulated at a much slower pace than it does today.

In the XX Century, the expansion of goods and services made available to a vigorous consumer's market - and, therefore, with increased competition – in addition to the diversification of the media (radio, TV, print media), resulted in the establishment of what we call Strategic Intelligence, that is, a set of coordinated actions to seek, treat and distribute useful information to support the decision-making process throughout the various levels of the organization's hierarchy.

The natural evolution was the establishment of the specialized consultancies' market. Such consultancies prepare scenarios and trends. The evolution also resulted in the establishment of pollsters and market research companies.

Globalization exponentially expanded the consumer's market, and also expanded the limits of competition amongst companies, changing old management concepts. The internet or web, upon facilitating access and the issue of information to billions of people, has caused and is causing a true evolution in the actual world – whatever the focus of the evaluation may be – which evidently includes the business environment.

One of these effects – actually a well-known one – is the exponential growth in information production and the speed at which it circulates (which had been restricted to the timing of TV, radio, the print media, and, certainly, fax, telegraph and postal services).

A study carried out by EMC^2, a leading company in the international data storage market, shows that, as of 2014, there were almost 1 septillion bits of information in a digital format – about the same number of known stars in the sky – available in the world and stored in computers, servers, smartphones and tablets. According to the same study, the forecast was that by 2020, this number would experience a sixfold increase at least.

Another effect was the broader democratization of access to information: in a little over a decade, the number of people with access to digital information jumped from the order of magnitude of tens of thousands to hundreds of millions. In Brazil only, according to the Instituto Brasileiro de Geografia e Estatística [Brazilian Geography and Statistics Institute] (IBGE), for an estimated population of 202 million people, 95.4 million (that is, 47 %) had access to the web in 2015. And we must stress that this access takes place both to obtain and to issue information.

The multiplication of the sources of information has also hit the fast lane, especially after the establishment of the social networks and the use of mobile devices that provide quick access to the web. This is the third direct effect of the internet: the action of groups of stakeholders (actors capable of influencing or being influenced by the organization's action), which was barely perceptible, now has a direct impact on the company's ability to implement its planning.

A typical example that took place recently in Brazil: the delays in the construction of the Belo Monte hydroelectric dam, due to the mobilization of the local communities – whose voice even mobilized groups of American and European environmental activists.

Another example: the erosion in the image of one of the largest companies in the world, engaged in the manufacture of sporting goods – resulting in decreased sales and a strategic change in course – due to media stories, published in 1996, disclosing the fact that the company was employing slave labor in Bangladesh. Since then, by means of concrete actions, this company has been trying to consolidate its image in the market as one of the most active organizations in combating slave labor.

Finally, as a result of all aforementioned factors, there is a fourth effect – so far less consolidated and analyzed, but just as important. We are now talking about the structural changes that the easy access to information, in addition to information technology's development, has caused in the production processes, in the business environment, and in the market structure.

Let us look at some elements of these quick changes that are already noticeable:

- In macroeconomics – the growth of the "sharing economy", which already involves billions of dollars in the United States and comprises the replacement of purchasing with renting, leasing, borrowing or sharing. With the passage of time – apparently not a long time – this trend may spread and significantly change behaviors in the consumer's market.
- In microeconomics, there is the consolidation of new businesses and products, which naturally results in erosion of other, time-honored, business and products. And we must stress that when we say "time-honored", we also include businesses that were started 20 or 30 years ago. The spread of WhatsApp – first for data communication, and more recently, voice communication, jeopardizes the cellphone carriers' income.
- In the audio-visual environment, Netflix competes with cable TV and movie theaters, since some distributors have refused to work with its productions, such as the 2015 feature film *Beast of no Nation*.
- In the urban transportation arena, Uber has significantly affected the "taxi" business. Its market value is in the order of magnitude of millions of dollars. Other examples are the websites that connect the consumer directly with the provider, as is the case with delivery services, and real estate brokerage – in which the physical need for a broker has been substantially decreased.
- Finally, in the interoperational sense, associated with productive processes, but also with a significant impact on the market, we have the "fourth industrial revolution", based on the "internet of things" whose

most basic definition is the digital connection amongst several devices. According to current studies, up to 2021, the internet of things tends to substantially change productive processes, the business environment, and the job market – with an estimated loss of 5 million jobs worldwide, which will also, and certainly, affect the consumer's market. The changes this may cause are so significant and blunt that the internet of things has even been amongst the major themes in the Davos Forum, early in 2016.

When we add, to the virtual environment data, those that circulate only through the actual world (for instance, backstage comments, print media, etc.), as well as the changes caused in the business environment, the amount of information made available to the organization becomes unfathomable. The challenge here is to set apart what is and what is not necessary to the organization's operation, and what may be of strategic value for its business. In other words, one has to find wheat in a mountain of chaff and turn it into food that encourages the company's "sustainable positioning" in the market. And one must notice that this happens in an environment in which everything may change in a matter of seconds!

This is where Strategic Intelligence comes into play, and, as part of it, IEAc.

According to IEAc, the Strategic Intelligence activity enables one to:

- Adapt to the changes, uncertainties and turbulence in one's environment;
- Define/conduct the organization's strategies according to its environment;

- Help the organization integrate information and knowledge in its products, services and decisions;
- Employ the organization's resources in a more adequate manner;
- Provide management with information that is useful for decision-making;
- Inform the organization's decision-making process: inform the decision (the intention to make a decision precedes the quest for information) and make a decision based on a piece of information (attention precedes the decision);
- Anticipate changes in order to take advantage of opportunities and prevent threats.

The professional approach for obtaining and reviewing anticipative information by means of the Anticipative and Collective Strategic Intelligence System does not preclude the time-honored trend analysis practices that have already been consolidated in the market, which result in the aforementioned benefits. It is added to them as yet another step towards perfecting the corporate Strategic Intelligence. It is, also, a direct result of the changes in the market, in the XXI Century, due to globalization and popularization of the internet.

And here we come up with a provocative question: was your company prepared for the changes in the business environment, caused by the web and by the evolution in information technology? How early was your company able to anticipate these phenomena? How should one interact with them?

If you produce soft drinks, for instance, wouldn't it be interesting to keep up with the discussions on the amount of sodium in your product?

If you produce milk-based foods, wouldn't it be interesting to know that people are talking about the fat and sugar indexes in the food that you produce? And what about the discussions on the effects of lactose?

Will gluten continue to be the athletes' number one enemy?

If you work in the defense industry, wouldn't it be interesting to know which way the next administration's investments will go?

What is going on today, in the regulatory environment? Are there any changes in the making? What effects would such changes bring to your business?

If you are engaged in agribusiness, what would be the implications of the regulations concerning the sale of real estate to foreign buyers?

Will the electric car really replace conventional vehicles? When is this going to happen? How much longer will you still be manufacturing combustion engine vehicles?

Do you manufacture motorcycles? Which way will the mobility issue go? What about the issues associated with living with the vehicles?

Are you in the fashion business? In addition to the next season's colors, is there anyone in the world performing some research on some kind of fabric that may bring a revolution to your business?

What lies ahead? What can I foresee? The responses are swirling around you. But the amount of information is so overwhelming that you do not have time to see it.

CHAPTER 4
JUST A MAN

> *"The winners will be those who restructure the manner in which the information flows in their business."*
>
> Bill Gates

The main executive in an organization, the CEO, whose job is to make decisions – often strategic ones – with regard to current and future issues, works in a lonely environment.

Of course, he is not an island. He is supported by a team – usually comprising advisors and executive assistants – which organizes his agenda, selects who he must see, and which is in charge of managing his agenda. He also receives information and reports from each area's vice-presidents or directors, and when applicable, he receives market surveys, opinion polls, political and economic scenarios, amongst so much other data.

As a result of his position, the CEO may, at any time of the day or night, convene the team of advisors, or the other executives, to clarify any issues or request data he may need.

Nevertheless, in spite of all this paraphernalia and corporate support resources, the CEO lives under the impression that he is alone: he can count on the fingers of one hand the number of people he can, in fact, trust, and to whom he can expose his doubts, weaknesses and insecurities, whether they are of a professional or personal nature. After all, he has become a hero, a myth – this image is part of the underpinnings of his career. And it is difficult, maybe impossible, for common mortals, to admit that their heroes also have Achilles' heels.

In general, the CEO wakes up early, exercises before sunrise is the first one in and the last one out – and, of course, everyone knows that. In addition, many CEOs dedicate their weekends to institutional activities and forget they are on a diet at the first cocktail in which they have the chance to talk business or do some networking. Optimistic by nature, visionaries by vocation, ambitious due to their education, determined by option, they are the ones who go to bed with the responsibility to guarantee jobs, profits, dividends, and protect the organization's reputation. They are also the ones who are supposed to foresee the future, anticipate the vulnerabilities, solve problems and guarantee the company's position in a market that is becoming more and more competitive. Therefore, on a daily basis, they face battles and try to win a war. Thus, the expression "to kill one lion every day" is commonplace in the corporate environment.

CEOs, therefore, hostages of the myth that was established around them – and that they helped build – call themselves "individuals who are responsible" for the companies' success and growth.

But, as is always the case, the myth does not match reality. The CEO is a common mortal, who, with a lot of effort, and oftentimes with great sacrifices, has worked his way up to the corner office. He, nevertheless, is not without his everyday chores, his insecurities, frustrations, affections, fears and challenges. He is a normal person, with his conquests, joys, jealousy, anger, merits, intelligence, successful operations, failures that might be kept under wraps, and, in addition, who has to work on a budget, who has to achieve results and meet goals, and who must undergo the board of directors' evaluation.

But who is the member of the closest or the most remote team, that can see that this superman, admired, and whose photographs appear on the covers of the leading business magazines, as well as in the newspapers, is nothing but a regular man, just like everyone else? This is what makes the CEO lonely. The loneliness is caused by his position – achieved with so much effort and desired by so many others – this causes difficulty in finding someone he can trust, in the workplace.

And, just like any common man, these supermen are cornered, on a daily basis, with a deluge of information that they must process and out of which they have to extract messages that point to the decision they must make within the next few minutes, the next few months, or the next few years. They are the ones who must identify the future's inaudible signals, usually hidden in the various areas within the organization – each one of them protecting itself in silos, with information that is essential to decision-making. After all, "information is power". That is another sentence that one often hears within the company's halls.

Harvard Business Review, Fortune, and other business management periodicals have been publishing articles that focus on the extremely awkward situation in which, currently, CEOs find themselves, especially those of large corporations. On one side, this is the result of the progress made by media outlets, which, minute by minute, make a vast and diversified range of information available. On the other side, the CEO's position is made difficult due to the transparency demands imposed by the shareholders and by society – these are demands whose intensity varies, depending on the area in which the company is active, and on its share capital structure.

The table shows the principles of corporate governance,

which are being imposed with increased rigor in the capital market. Think of the implications of the transparency practices, with so much sensitive data associated with the business. Think of how complex the equity issue is, considering the diversity of the groups associated with and/or interested in the business. But think, also, how much you have to know about the people you are talking with – their movements, their desires, their interests, and their power – to ensure all these groups are treated in a fair and equitable manner.

CORPORATE GOVERNANCE PRINCIPLES

Transparency (*disclosure*)	Effective channels to disclose information, not only in-house but also as far as third-parties are involved
Equity (*fairness*)	Fair and equitable treatment amongst all classes of partners and with regard to related and/or stakeholders
Accountability	Proof of separation of interests as far as the company's and personal interests are concerned (those of management or equity holders)
Compliance	
Ethics	
Corporate Responsibility	
Corporate governance: the management field that deals with the set of relationships amongst companies' management, their boards of directors, their shareholders and other stakeholders. It establishes the roadmap according to which the companies' equity holders have their return on investment assured	

Source: Instituto Brasileiro de Governança Corporativa / IBGC (Brazilian Institute of Corporate Governance)

And pay attention: the responsibility with regard to society is so much greater, as one would expect, as far as public services corporations, or those that serve numerous clients, are concerned. These companies' CEOs, especially, are naturally exposed to a lot of pressure, which may originate not only from the board of directors and from the more well-known stakeholders (such as clients, suppliers, employees and shareholders), but also from the government, from regulatory agencies, and, in some cases, from international entities.

Under these circumstances, the worst-case scenario, according to the experts, is that the CEO may establish an armor around himself, based on extreme self-assurance. Such armour makes him unwilling to accept initiatives that lead to the quest for information, or snippets of information that may be of value to the organization's guidance.

Actually, even without this armor, the CEO, try as he might, will not, unless he has an organized and effective support system, have an overview of what is going on all levels of his company, or in the market in which it operates, so as to be able to face, in an effective manner, the issues he is up against.

Even his trusted advisors or consultants may only help him to a certain extent. This is because, when they employ the time-honored information acquisition and analysis standards, they are able to forecast trends and scenarios. Nevertheless, they seldom foresee movements that lead to ruptures – which are being seen more and more often in information society – since their eyes are trained to look into the past in order to forecast the future, and not to seek snippets of the present that will enable them to foresee events different from those that the market, as a whole, forecasts.

Thus, the CEO's great challenge, at the present juncture, is to acquire specific and strategic information that will enable him to consolidate the organization in a constantly changing environment. In the industrial society, what made the difference was the possession of production assets. In the information society, what makes the difference is the access to strategic information that is made available to everyone, but that only a few are able to see – and understand!

How can one obtain such information?

"The winners will be those who restructure the manner in which the information flows in their business", stated Bill Gates. A prophecy, more than a heads-up: the winners are those who are aware of the evidence that the human mind, especially when it works alone, in a lonely environment, is not able to choose, select, filter, verify, classify and organize all the information that is indispensable in order to be able to evaluate the following steps.

Thus, whereas technology surprises us with its advancement in geometric progression, the good old dose of humility will favor the decision-makers who know how to listen to the information noises. The answers will always be there, in your own company, or in a nearby external environment, kept under lock and key, by those who know that information is power. But power actually will be with the manager who is able to make everyone shares what they know, to everyone's benefit.

With ever-increasing speed and regularity, technology provides information that enables one to foresee *tsunamis* and opportunities for the organization. It is up to people to acquire such information, analyze it and share, forgoing an immediate individual benefit, and instead choosing an immediate and long-term collective benefit.

In the information society, forecasting the future by looking at the rearview mirror, as is usually the case with scenarios' forecasts or opinion poll analysis, is not enough. By the same token, acting according to the teachings of the best business schools is also not enough, since the revolution will come of something, still hidden, one that has just been detected by the advances in information technology;

consumers with the power to destroy a company's reputation by means of a click through the social networks; (true or false) news that may sabotage the value of a company's shares in the Stock Exchange; isolated communities in the middle of a forest, that may cause delays in an infrastructure construction schedule. This is to name just a few examples.

"Instead of the rearview mirror, companies should be using a spyglass", says Vitor Madeira, a member of our preliminary team and now IBM-Brazil vice-president, and a Business Intelligence specialist. There are three major challenges in this case:

- One must be nimble enough to be able to sense, rapidly, the possibilities of changes in the business environment;
- One must make sure the information gathered is incorporated to an organized and logical system, comprising weak and strong signals, which will enable the CEO to widen his field of vision so that he can see facts that will possibly take place in the future and that may disrupt trends;
- One must put together an in-house structure, comprising people – with the aid of software – who know the business and that strive to consolidate this organized and logical system in the organization's daily routine.

Once these three requirements are met, the CEO will be ready to see what no one else sees and make decisions that may ensure the organization's medium-term and long-term competitiveness and sustainability. Thus, in most cases, his actions will make it possible to make the best of the opportunities and prevent crises in the market.

According to Madeira, for the decision-making process, many companies have been employing information technology (IT), software to collect data on clients, sales, production costs, financial transactions, legal and operational issues, etc. As a result, they have a vast amount of data that can be called "operational or influential data". Nevertheless, such data are not a headlight, not something that makes a difference. Such data work in a different fashion, as compared with Anticipation Data, as we stated in Chapter 2.

In other words: these companies do not have the tools to process information in an intelligent manner. Therefore, they do not have anything like what is known today as business intelligence or its variants in the specialized jargon, such as competitive intelligence or environmental scanning.

In addition, these processes usually require days or months to be completed. This speed is inadequate, considering the pace at which information circulates in the market. Therefore, the conclusion one reaches due to these analyses will be obsolete from day one.

Corporations usually also count on consultancies which analyze macroeconomic trends or the political scene, and, based on such analyses, they provide forecasts. The awareness of these scenarios is of great value and must not be cast aside. But it is not enough.

Moments of crisis or moments at which fast-paced changes take place demand that such information be seen as part of a wide-ranging context, which also encompasses the material disclosed by other sources, such as social networks, the perception of in-house professionals, the press, comments on the market and moves by the competition. These data will provide a more complete picture of the here-and-now situation as well as of future possibilities.

An example of how trends forecasts are not enough to provide a wider view is the behavior of the Brazilian consumer market in 2015/16, when a precipitous and wide-ranging drop in sales took place, due to the macroeconomic situation, the loss or purchasing power and the consumers' lack of confidence. The trend was forecast in practically all scenario studies. Nevertheless, few of such surveys pointed to the possibility of growth of a few specific businesses.

One of these businesses was the car repair shops segment, which took advantage of the drop in new car sales. Another was the natural foods segment. In the latter, the consumer, not only decided to spend less on traditional products, due to the loss of purchasing power, but also replaced traditional products with more healthy items, joining the trend, that came about a few years back, and that has been on the increase due to the adverse state of the economy, whereby people are seeking better health and quality of life.

Finally, a third case was the one seen in the premium category of cleaning products. It is important to note that, at the beginning of that same year, a new law was sanctioned which regulated domestic labor. That has increased the hiring and maintenance costs of this type of employee, while at the same time there was a decrease in the middle class' purchasing power. Result: a significant number of households replaced salaried employees with others, hired on a per diem basis, and employers started performing some of the domestic labor chores, choosing premium products to facilitate the work.

Without a doubt, the company that examined and analyzed the microeconomics signals made available in the market was able to take more advantage of the opportunities than those that only focused on the macro trends. It is not a coincidence that the year saw the roll-out and the growth of diet and light food brands, and the diversification of cleaning products (including the diversification of rubber and latex glove brands and models, as one can attest by looking at the supermarket gondolas) and even the rebirth of companies that specialize in home cleaning.

Incidentally, some of these companies started advertising through the social networks almost simultaneously with the issue of the domestic labor law. Considering that a business structuring and the hiring of the relevant team of professionals require at least a few months' lead time, one can conclude that these entrepreneurs were aware of the weak signals that were giving a heads-up on specific opportunities in the midst of a general crisis.

As Raquel Janissek-Muniz wrote, the anticipative nature of a piece of information does not mean anticipation in the sense that one is able to foresee or establish a trend. Forecasting and trending oftentimes are associated with the idea of reviewing the past to foresee the future, on the assumption that there will be continuity in behaviors. The anticipating nature, which the specialist emphasizes, is about innovation. "Many times, snippets of data may bear the seeds of innovation, which may eventually mean disrupture", she wrote. Detecting this possibility of disrupture will enhance not only the establishment but also the review of corporate strategies.

While still focusing on the Brazilian market's behavior in 2015/16, one can think of an established industrialized food company. Surveys indicate a general decrease in demand, which includes this company's products. The occasional product may be affected due to the price, in a slow or slowing market. What the company finds out is that the consumer does not reject the product in and of itself, due to its quality standards, but is simply buying less in order to decrease expenses, that is, the consumer is establishing a new situation in the market. How can the scenario be managed?

Decreasing the margin is never an option, since the company will not sacrifice its already low profitability. Promotions have a temporary effect. A new, more ambitious, marketing action may promote the products. Nevertheless, a reduction in output, and a slash in payroll is almost the route taken.

What else could the company do under these circumstances?

A jingle aired by a major TV network goes something like this: "If you ask the wrong question, do not expect to hear the right answer".

In this case there is no wrong question. The issue here is that the answers are generally sought only through the time-honored methods, that is, scenarios' analysis and opinion polls. To innovate in this search, looking also into the weaker signals – or the for the parallel clues – may result in innovative answers. For instance: if the company is engaged in the industrialized food sector and is aware of the consumer's movement towards health and quality of life, it has information that makes it possible for it to decide if, while seeking to boost sales, it will adapt some of its production assets in order to roll out healthier products, such as lactose-free milk derivatives or a line of light treats and chocolates.

It is evident that the establishment of a similar strategy calls for stating the issue and obtaining information from a number of departments within the company, such as operations, marketing, communications, legal, etc. And this demands integration and communication amongst the areas – one of the main features of an organized and systematic system for the collection and analysis of market signals.

A painful example not related to the corporate environment but to public safety, shows how essential this integration is.

After the September 11, 2001 attacks on the World Trade Center twin towers, in New York, a great debate took place in the U.S. about the shortcomings of the country's public safety system. The information obtained attested to the fact that the Central Intelligence Agency (CIA) had information on two suspect activists then living in San Diego, California. The Federal Bureau of Investigation (FBI), in turn, had been monitoring the actions taken by a group of Saudi individuals who initiated flight training in Florida.

One thing was certain: the agencies did not share the information they had. If they had share them it could have prevented the terrorist attack? This is a question the remains in the realm of assumptions. But the fact is that, after September 11, information on potential terrorists in the U.S. started being interchanged amongst domestic safety agencies, in close cooperation with other countries' intelligence agencies. And since then, no other large terrorist attack has taken place in the United Sates.

Another important characteristic for the company that intends to work with the market's weaker signals is that it must have a well organized in-house structure. In this case, one would recommend the support of strategic communication agencies, whose scope of work has been expanded within the last few years, adding, to the establishment and consolidation of image and reputation, the provision, to the client, of strategic market information.

Hence, the need for the company to develop its one intelligence system, which must be interpreted as a participative decision-making process, which will ultimately, lands on the CEO's desk.

In order to put together a strategy, a useful thing to do is to analyze the feedback, that is, the reaction, on the part of the consumers, the competition, and the community itself, with regard to the actions taken by the company. The manager may also present the problem to a number of departments within his company and obtain, as feedback, some information that may be of value in the decision-making process, establishing a flow that cannot be watertight, but must be continuous as time goes by. Within this experience, we indicate that all of this may be more valuable to the extent that the various levels within the organization operate in sintony with its communication company.

With the evolution of the means of communication in a globalized world, large corporations cannot, therefore, stick to formulas that may have been safe in the past, but are inadequate to face current and future challenges. This new perception has triggered a cognitive interaction process that has been the object of study in a number of developed countries, opening spaces in the Anticipated and Collective Strategic Intelligence (IEAc) system (about which we have already written in Chapter 2).

IEAc, as described by Professor Lesca, "is a collective, proactive and continuous system, whereby the company's associates collect (in a voluntary manner) and use pertinent information with regard to their environment and the changes that may occur in it, seeking to create business opportunities, innovate, adapt to (and even anticipate) the environment's evolution, prevent unpleasant strategic surprises and reduce risks and uncertainties in general".

One must make it quite clear that this system is not meant to collect information that may lead to "gambling" in the stock market, to industrial espionage, or to any other activity that may not be considered legitimate. Participative and Anticipative Intelligence is a corporate governance instrument, and, therefore, it meets current compliance criteria, so as to prevent any ethics-related conflict.

An image of the work to be developed within the company, according to the studies promoted by Professors Lesca and Raquel Janissek-Muniz, is that of the radar, an instrument for detection and ranging of a remote object, fairly commonplace nowadays, invented over a century ago and perfected by British scientists early in World War II.

A company's radar is a device to acquire and obtain information, a gesture of attention and awareness with regard to the company's in-house and external environment. According to the authors, one can also see radar as an interrogation, both with regard to information that may help the company achieve its goals, acting as a prospection instrument in its environment, as well with its ability to interpret information that has already been obtained.

By the same token, one must stress that the company must ascertain the confidentiality of the information it possesses. In order to work in a holistic, integrated manner, as pointed out by Vitor Madeira, the company has to have, at its disposal, mechanisms for the preservation of the most sensitive data for its operation, and that cannot be disclosed outside of its environment.

Any wider-ranging and more structured intelligence system must have tools to distinguish what is and what is not confidential information. This filter is indispensable for the security of its operations, as well as for the maintenance of the reputation that the company has in the market and with regard to society in general.

We still have some time before robots are able to replace human's ability to read the obvious between the lines. Incidentally, Vitor Madeira reports that IBM developed a product named Watson – a reference to the doctor who worked as Sherlock Holmes' assistant –, the first artificial intelligence software in the world to help doctors diagnose patients. Using Anticipative Intelligence we may even foresee that it won't be long before a more evolved version of Watson may have a more prominent role in the CEO's spacious offices.

This set of research and up-to-date theoretical studies, added to our market expertise acquired due to the work with our clients have enabled to us to develop an exclusive Participative Intelligence system, which we will describe at length in the next chapter.

CHAPTER 5

A SIMPLE, LOW-COST AND INTELLIGENT STRUCTURE

"In a universe made of energy, everything is interconnected, everything is one."

BRUCE H. LIPTON

The basic premises of the previous chapters may be summarized as follows:

- Access to and analysis of Anticipative Information for decision-making are strategic for corporate competitiveness and sustainability;
- The strategic attribute grows exponentially to the extent that the web and the services and products made available by the web are consolidated and cause deep ruptures in the market and in the business environment;
- Given the huge amount of data that the web makes available to the user, the Century XXI challenge is no longer finding information, but, rather, selecting the information that is of strategic interest to the organization;
- In order to add useful items to corporate decision-making, such search and analysis may not result from individual initiative, but from an organized structure, comprising people and software.

If you liked the premises and the thesis and if you get organized to insert these practices in the organization, the next step is to prepare the relevant budget forecast proposal, to be submitted in the next management meeting, put together a department, hire professionals who specialize in data monitoring and analysis, using late-model computers. Wrong! Seeking and analyzing, in an organized manner, the market's weak signals, is much cheaper than one might think.

Thus, forget the futuristic scenes with dozens of technology nerds, sitting in front of computers, stationed in a base out there in the middle of a desert, entrusted with a single mission: to gather data made available through the web – something similar to what one would see in *Spectre*, the James Bond movie.

Instead, think about the possibility to train "the eyes" of professionals that are already working in a number of areas within the organization, to, with the advice of consultants who specialize in information management, search for market data, share such data amongst themselves, and, as a result of such sharing, draw conclusions and subsidies that are useful for decision-making. Of course, this takes place online, with the support of specific software.

This is the proposition in connection with CBI (Cellular Business Intelligence), a system developed in Brazil, by MSL Group, totally dedicated to the acquisition and analysis of such information – or weak signals – without, of course, neglecting the stronger information. The use of this system takes place by employing a simple software product, and turns it into a competitive differential for the client to establish corporate strategies and meet the requirements for reputation building and consolidation.

CBI is a permanent structure, across the board, within the company, comprising, as we have already stated, a multi-functional team, supported by a software product, that operates online. Its goal is to maintain a continuous scanning process within the business environment. These are some of the questions that may be answered by CBI:

- How to make inroads into new specific markets?
- How is our brand perceived and what are the main threats it faces?
- What competitors are the main threats we face?
- How can we defend ourselves against new and disruptive businesses?
- What are our businesses' critical themes?
- How can we operate in the market so as to expand our business?
- How can regulation affect our business in the medium and long term?
- How can we forecast our clients requirements' trends?

CBI's structure is inspired in the cell operating structure concept, originating from biologist Bruce H. Lipton's teachings.

Let us now go over the main messages of this concept, which we have mentioned in Chapter 1:

- Thousands of stimuli in motion;
- A constant quest for the most adequate answers;
- Survival instinct;
- Teamwork;
- Exponential increase in situational awareness;
- Workload subdivision.

Any resemblance to what we have said so far about data acquisition, selection, and analysis within the organization is not purely coincidental!

Comparing CBI to the cell concept, one can say that the system works like a team in which each professional works like a cell, which interacts with the other cells, exponentially increasing the quantity of data sought in the environment, selecting the most adequate answers, and based on the latter, reaching conclusions. Thus, situational awareness grows exponentially and, in time, ensures the organization's sustainability and competitiveness.

CBI is provided with two complementary cellular structures, in constant interaction, which possess the knowledge required for weak signals acquisition and business environment analysis. One of them is organic to the client company. It comprises professionals of a number of areas such as marketing, logistics, supply, finance, new business, communication, etc. Therefore, they have a deep knowledge of the business and are able to see it from different perspectives. The other is an external one, which performs environment scanning, comprising senior professionals who specialize in information issue, transmission, reception and management.

This complementary knowledge allows not only for data mining, but, mainly, for the selection of what is, in fact, important for the company. The two cellular structures work in an integrated manner and online, due to the support provided by the software, developed specifically for this purpose. In other words: structures operate at a speed that is compatible with the speed at which information circulates in society, both in the virtual environment and in actual life.

Any member of one of the cellular structures may provide the group with a piece of information that he or she feels is of interest to the organization. Thus, as opposed to what occurs when the areas work as watertight compartments, the sales professional may come across important data in the supply area, the communication representative may become aware of what is happening in the finance area. Such data have both individual, and especially, collective value. Their integration and analysis by the team members originate the required conclusions that will enable one to make a difference for the organization within the market.

As is usually the case with ad agencies, research organizations and many others, CBI creates space for brainstorming. The difference is that such brainstorming is not limited to face-to-face meetings, held at regular intervals, about specific issues. CBI takes place continuously, within a virtual environment, complemented by periodical, face-to-face meetings, and encompasses the whole scope of the organization's actuation, as the previously questions show.

CBI as a whole, therefore, centers on the "human factor" – that is, the professionals' ability to open their eyes and ears to the market and turn the data they receive into analysis of strategic value to the organization. Technological evolution and information technology support the process. As we stated in the previous chapter, technology surprises us exponentially every minute, but it takes humility for one to be able to hear information's noises. And only human beings are able to listen, look and think.

One of the first steps after the decision is made is the preparation of the team of professionals who will participate in the CBI to acquire information, map the environments in which the client company is active and map the relevant stakeholders (for further detail, see the last item in this chapter). These are the data that, throughout the process, are turned into strategic information.

One must make it clear that this activity does not mean one more task in the professional's day-to-day routine: it is inserted into the organization's culture. After the "eye" is trained, information is acquired naturally, while normal activities are performed. For instance, in the course of a social event, or a business meeting, while one is reading the papers or listening to backstage comments, amongst other situations. The most required actions will be quick: the entry of the data acquired in the software, which is similar to the now-commonplace entry of posts in the social networks.

Picture yourself on Facebook or LinkedIn, posting personal or professional messages. For instance, pictures taken during a birthday party or during recent vacations, on the mountains or on the beach, or information on the new product your company has rolled out. Accessing CBI's software is not much different. As a matter of fact, we call it a portal.

As is the case with Facebook or LinkedIn, CBI's portal hosts a restricted group of "friends". It is provided with a sophisticated security system and requires authorization and password for access. These "friends", located simultaneously within an in-house and an external cell, are the ones who acquire and exchange information on the various issues the company is interested in.

The data-mining agent him or herself provides the information entered with tags. This makes it possible to cross-check and synthesizes the material acquired by the various agents and, in time, enables the establishment of a large, organized, and shared database, comprising information that is relevant and of strategic value to the organization.

- Information originating from various sources – including the virtual environment and actual life.
- Influencers' (stakeholders') maping.
- Sharing of information acquired.

- Support during analysis: identification of the information that is inter-related.
- Coordination – team members are encouraged to participate.

All these data can be accessed by all team members. In addition to them, the intelligence cell coordination (usually a company professional) may monitor the participation of each member, establish which ones are active, and with such additional data, evaluate the individual's performance as well as the cell's overall performance.

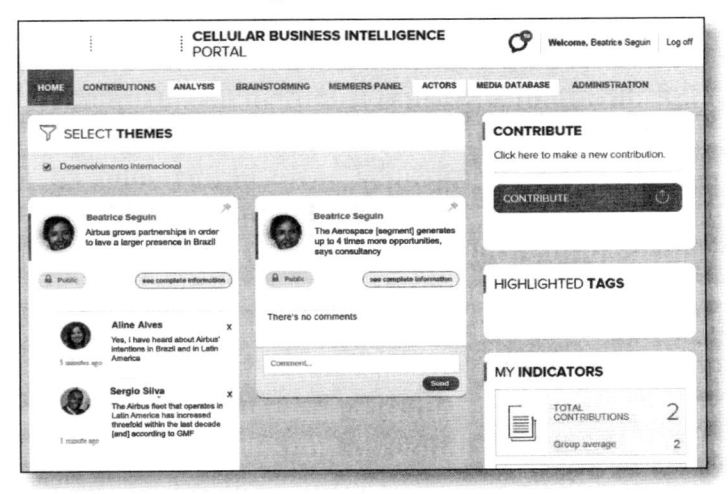

So far we have been talking about information. We must bear it in mind that information is produced by people. People, who, like you and I, think, feel, act, react, comment, purchase and make decisions. Any business, whatever its origin and purpose may be, is made by people and for people.

When gathered into specific groups, with some kind of relationship with organizations, people are called stakeholders. Stakeholders are, in fact, the organization's underpinnings. The organization, after all, will not survive without its network, encompassing clients, suppliers, shareholders, in-house professionals, regulatory agencies, competition, and community, amongst others.

One term that is becoming more common, and that is used to refer to stakeholders, is "influencers" – that is, groups that, either directly or indirectly, are influenced by the organization and exercise influence over it. Their actions may favor or compromise the business plan's implementation.

Since these groups' members issue information and spread it around, their monitoring, and whenever possible, the anticipation of their steps are also crucial for the decision-making process. This is why they are the object of monitoring and analysis by CBI.

The portal has a specific field for the analysis of the main representatives of these influencers' groups, with four classification criteria:

- Power to exercise influence and decision-making power over the business;
- Positioning (for or against the organization and the issues the organization is engaged in);
- The extent and reach of their power to exercise influence;
- Degree of relationship to the company.

This resource makes it possible to constantly map the groups and their relevant representatives and, as a result, provides a clearer view of those who can cause a positive or negative impact on the business. Therefore, it facilitates, a great deal, the management of the organization's various relationships.

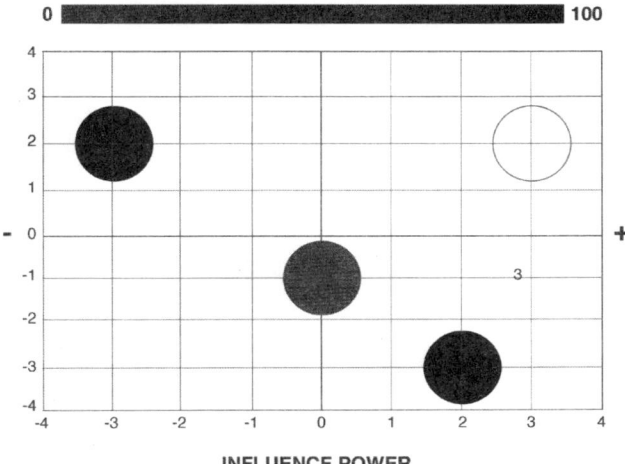

It is also noteworthy that, as far as the relationships are concerned, evolutions and ruptures may take place in time. Groups and individuals, who, at the moment, represent a threat, by reacting to an approach, may become allies in the future. By the same token, groups that support a given issue may become its opponents. Furthermore, one has to consider the change in the influential and decision-making power with the passage of time. Groups, that currently exercise a great influential power – being therefore, a corporate strategy priority – may, in the future, be replaced with other influencers, who are more sensitive to the moment's decision.

As is the case with information proper, CBI makes it possible to have a dynamic view of these groups, by issue and with the passage of time: the evolution of their position and the comparison of such position with that of other influencers. That is a view that makes it possible not only to manage current issues, but also provides the basis for long-term corporate strategy.

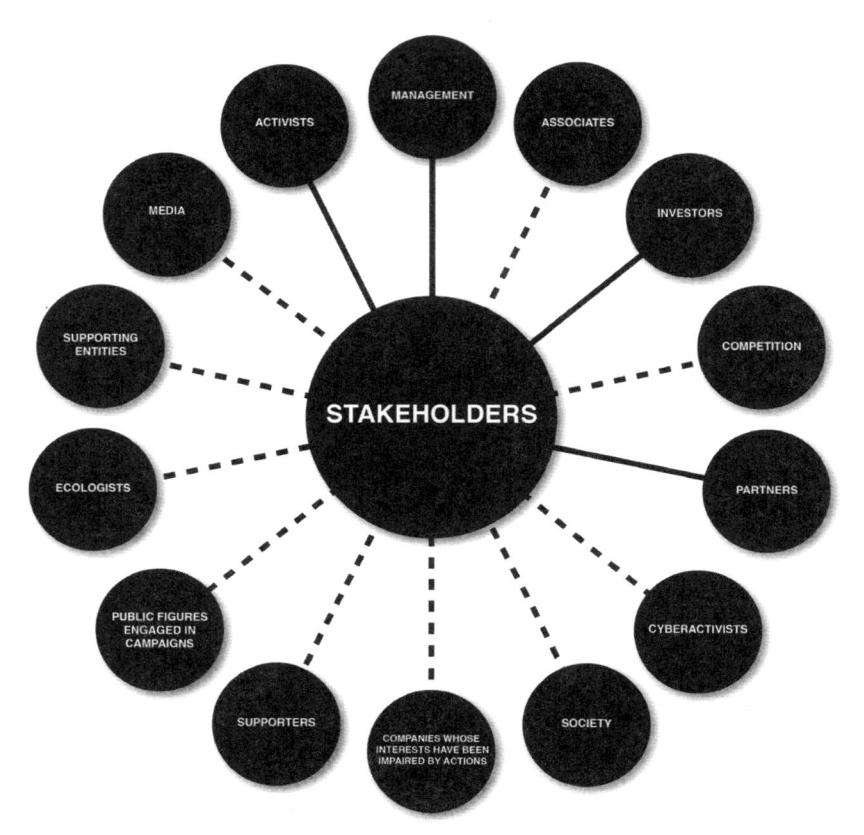

Above, as an example, an international environmental protection NGO, active in over 40 countries schematic map. You may notice the diversity of influencers with whom the NGO relates. Our question: does your company have a similar map? Is it nimble and useful enough to capture current movements and the possibility of future movements by means of relationship management?

CHAPTER 6
THE DIFFERENTIAL IN CELLULAR BUSINESS INTELLIGENCE - CBI

> "Smart cells become increasingly intelligent."
> BRUCE H. LIPTON

The creation of intelligence cells, intended to seek and analyze weak signals in the market, is the first step for the change in corporate culture. With action across the board, within the organization, your activities may not only cause an impact in the present, but will also work as a guiding light for the direction to be taken in the future, provided, of course, it yields visible and measurable results, that is: it must be successful with the passage of time.

To sum up, what we propose with the Intelligence Cells is the replacement of the boundaries – that prevent information from flowing within the company – with an organized system that includes these signals' acquisition and analysis within the corporations' day-to-day routine. The main issue, therefore, is the organized and responsible democratization of knowledge. In other words: the establishment of a structure comprising a software product (as explained in the previous chapter) and people willing to include this practice into the organization's day-to-day routine.

And, if there is democratization, there is also the replacement of old and conservative practices with a new attitude. Here are a few examples of practices related to this "new thing":

- To induce various areas, which historically tend to clam up, to integrate with other areas;
- To encourage the establishment of multifunctional teams, not only in specific situations (crises or opportunities), but in day-day operations;
- To prevent information from being presented on specific occasions only, such as management meetings or interviews with the CEO.

It is a fact, after all, that in the corporate environment, in general, the interchange of information takes place only on very specific occasions. For instance, when there is a crisis that affects the company, directly or indirectly, when multifunctional meetings are held in order to establish actions to be taken or a public event involving the attendance of the CEO, directors or vice-presidents, communications, legal, finance, marketing, operational areas, etc.

It is also a fact that, on these occasions, surprisingly, data or information that had been kept under wraps by one or more departments comes to light. Had this information been made available beforehand, it could have been of great value to prevent the problem at hand. The question is that, after the fact, everything goes back to the previous status: areas clam up; multifunctional teams are disbanded; and the barriers that prevent the free flow of information are rebuilt.

Companies that engage in this practice are not aware of the importance of the daily and systematic flow of information amongst the areas, for their sustainability and competitiveness in the market. It is a matter of culture.

Intelligence Cells have the power to change this archaic culture.

Nevertheless, we know that these cells' implementation is a complex task. "The decision-makers see IEAc (Anticipative and Collective Strategic Intelligence) as a difficult process. Simon and Kern (2001) stress the fact that the implementation is also seen as an important organizational change, and thus, the organization's employees resist and refuse to cooperate. Simpson, in turn, stated that the associates involved are unable to understand the goal and the usefulness of intelligence processes", says Raquel Janissek-Muniz, in a detailed article on "Critical Factors in Anticipative and Collective Strategic Intelligence".

Based on academic studies, market polls and her own consultancy experience, the professor consolidates, in this article, the main critical factors in an IEAc cell and acknowledges the fact that her list "does not purport be the ultimate list", but it enables the reader to have an overview of the challenges to be faced when one takes the initiative to develop and implement such a process". After all, this concept is a new one. It transcends the work that the traditional consultancy and advisory outfits provide, to boost companies' productivity and competitiveness.

So, the CBI model we came up with is dynamic and evolutionary. In addition, according to which the IEAc method is preached, it is structured and kept as a collective effort, since it will engage a number of in-house professionals as well as outsourced consultants, contributing to the required cultural change so that information may be democratized.

The main thing, nevertheless, is everyone's active participation in putting solutions together. This means one has to give up the comfort zone of frozen methodologies, which are the market's mainstay, and engage in a dynamic and creative process. Its core is the continuous and organized interchange of information between the cell that acquires information in the outside environment and the cell within the company itself. Its purpose is the joint detection and implementation of the solutions for the challenges found.

For avoidance of doubt, it is a good idea to clarify that the outside cell that performs environment scanning does not work only with data stored in a database, the so-called big data. Its raw material is qualified information, which is spread around in the market. Such information is reviewed and cross-checked with the aid of the software we created, thus making it possible to share it constantly, along with the conclusions obtained worldwide by an international network of outsourced consultants.

They communicate constantly by means of interfaces, providing stimulae for the process of weak or strategic signals perception, to produce results for the organization, such as employees' encouragement and increased productivity, improvement in the ability to deal with information (which is often ambiguous and uncertain), and involving subtle changes. After all, these cells are fully engaged in all steps of the processes that may lead to the decision-making by the company's CEO or president.

Whereas, within the company, cells are made up by employees from a number of areas, within the outside consultancy, we will maintain a team that specializes in working with information, public relations and corporate management. We will work jointly, collecting data, analyzing and sharing information associated with strategic issues for each company, which is based on the premise that closed silos or niches will be broken, since these are the characteristics of an obsolete corporate culture, which makes it impossible for information to be shared, as it should be, amongst the various areas.

First of all, one must establish, in a wide-ranging view, the strategic issues to be monitored by the Intelligence

Cells. The selection involves the most sensitive issues for the company or those it sees as a risk, weakness, threat and opportunity. The range selected may be a wide one, from logistic shortcomings to the roll-out of a new product, for instance.

To that end, the outsourced consultants meet with the company's president and/or executives selected by him/her, in order to become familiar with the vital issues in the present and in the foreseeable future, as perceived by the client. This discussion, that must be as wide-ranging as possible, makes it possible for one to establish the issues one considers of strategic importance.

It is the president's job to select the areas to be visited, in addition to the directors, advisors and professionals to be interviewed. In addition, the company shall decide who will be selected to comprise the Intelligence Cell that shall be structured within its workforce.

The outsourced consultancy recommends that this be a multifunctional and cognitive team, amongst other features. This issue shall be dealt with in further detail within the next chapter. The outsourced consultancy has a specialized team in the treatment of information, anticipative intelligence, public relations and corporate management, strategic knowledge areas for the work to be developed.

In the next step, the outsourced consultancy will establish which economic agents (consumers, competition, representatives of the three tiers of government) that, thereinafter, will be referred to as "players". This definition is directly associated with the identification of the strategic or priority issues from the company's point of view. These are the issues that will provide the guidelines for the search for information, and, certainly, for the monitoring of the players capable of issuing it, receiving it, and transmit it.

All information with regard to such players must be carefully reviewed, especially if it appears as weak signals.

The timeframe forecast for this cycle is two days. That is long enough for the preparation of the list of items object of the study, and definition of the players object of attention. Within a week, all members of the Intelligence Cells will probably have been appointed. A key figure of this team, appointed by the company, is the operations head or coordinator, that is, the individual in charge of information acquisition and analysis, throughout the process. He or she will work in close cooperation with a high-level professional with the outsourced consultancy. Both will be the managers or coordinators for the system's implementation.

Once the process is under way, the professionals appointed as the company's Intelligence Cell members must undergo a training process. In spite of the fact that they have had years of experience in the sector or in the company, they may have had little or no previous contact with information work – especially anticipative information.

This training is to make sure they pay attention to the detection of weak signals, in addition to the market's current information. This, however, does not mean they will attend all Intelligence Cell meetings. For starters, they will only serve as the company's "antennas" in the market.

The best way to go about this is to select a group of 20 professionals within a number of areas, preferably those whose curiosity or interest for information stands out. Thus, it is worth pointing out that one should not use, as a requirement for joining the group, the individual's position in the company's organizational chart. Department heads, even those who hold key positions, such as finance, production and sales, are not necessarily the best choices. They may not have the proper skills set and may not have the time to engage in this task – which demands quite a bit of hands-on time (for further details on the participants' qualifications and characteristics, refer to the next chapter).

The acquisition of information with regard to the issues and players identified represent's CBI's tasks square one. At this juncture, as said by Lesca and Janissek-Muniz, 2015, it is worth pointing out that the weak signals may present themselves:

- In snippets, lacking all information on the event that may be forecast;
- Spread out amongst the clutter of useless data that may prevent their identification. A weak signal is not easily visible and most people are unable to pinpoint it;
- Difficult to detect, since they are immersed in messy data;
- Ambiguous, since they may be seen in a number of ways. They are unclear, ambivalent;
- Unexpected/surprising, since they are found by happenstance, unpredicted, unfamiliar, often not repetitive, and therefore, may go unnoticed;
- Uncertain, due to the uncertainty generated by the information;
- Inaccurate, due to the vague meaning;
- Not deliberate, due to the fact that the signal's issuer had not intended to issue it;
- Incomplete, since the information requires other data in order to make any sense;
- Their usefulness is not perceived, since, apparently, their meaning is weak;
- They are hardly pertinent, since we do not know how to connect them to a piece of information or how to categorize it with regard to current issues; by the same

token we do not know who could be interested in such data.

A good example of a weak signal was a story that seemed to be of no importance but that ended up having significant impact, about the hiring of a female purchasing director by a certain company (for obvious reasons we will not mention names here).

A French newspaper published a story according to which a female executive from XYZ company would be appointed sales director for the EFG group. This seemed like a routine story seen in a business-oriented newspaper – it mentioned an appointment, it did not provide any details, and thus the information did not seem to be of any use. It could even have been published to please an advertiser, which is relatively commonplace in the media. The reaction in the market was practically non-existent: 100 purchasing area professionals were interviewed, and none of them had read the newspaper story.

This low-visibility piece of information – and possibly undetected, or, if it was read, it was dismissed by the competition – had, nevertheless, an important outcome in the market. It paved the way for significant changes in the EFG group, which, four years later took the following steps:

- Implemented a 30% reduction in the number of suppliers;
- Developed an e-business strategy, which, within a year, enabled 20% of all purchases to be made online;
- Established, as a goal, to make 100% of purchases from low-cost countries.

Thus the question is: couldn't these facts and the

impact they caused in the market have been foreseen by the competition, if it had employed the Intelligence Cells method?

The example is not an assumption. It is an actual story that involved two large retail-sector companies. What happened was that company XYZ did not become aware of the information provided by the newspaper, or, if it did, it did not take it into consideration, and ended up on the losing side of the equation. If it had employed the tools provided by CBI, it could have taken the necessary steps in order to adapt to the new set of circumstances, using a more up-to-date operating procedure and streamlining its management to keep its market share.

The process for weak signals analysis data mining by means of the CBI may be summarized in two steps. One must point out, however, that these steps may take weeks or months, depending on the importance given to the information, its relevance to corporate strategy and its complexity. The steps are as follows:

1. Determine who can benefit from this information, what is its potential to cause changes in the market – now or in the future. It is important to point out that the meaning of these signals may be different for companies that have different positions in the market. (Considering the example, the news of the female executive's hiring would be a threat to local competition and suppliers, but it would be an opportunity to suppliers from countries with lower production costs.)

2. Try to figure out and understand what is behind this information. In the case of the female executive's hiring, the possible situations that could be foreseen would be:

- The hiring company wants to substantially change its purchasing policy;

- The hiring company wants to reduce costs by rationalizing purchasing or getting rid of some suppliers;
- This hiring indicates significant changes in the purchasing process.

CBI collection process

The acquisition process must involve at least one person from each key area within the company and one outsourced consultant, who will be in charge of monitoring the social networks and the media (both on and offline) with regard to all issues and players (competition, for instance). All these data miners enter and share the information acquired in the CBI software. The two Intelligence Cells coordinators (from the company and from the outsourced consultancy) will have access to all information entered. The time required for the completion of this cycle is estimated to be 10 to 12 days.

As we have stated previously, the CBI method is supported by a software product that has been especially developed by the outsourced consultancy in order to make data acquisition, sharing and analysis more nimble. Thus, the Intelligence Cells operating within the company and at the outsourced consultancy will be able to provide information to this platform, which facilitates the participation of all project members.

The software's main functionalities are:

- A database from several sources (media, market, influencers, etc.);
- Real-time data sharing;
- Collective information analysis;
- Support to the analysis of information placed on the platform (information cross-checking);

- Information mapping;
- Coordination and encouragement as far as participation is concerned.

The players' mapping is an important functionality, since it meets a clients' concern with regard to the management and quality of its relationship with the main stakeholders' groups. We must point out that such mapping is not static. It reflects each player's position, and the quality of its relationship with the company both now and as time goes by. This will not only enable the establishment of a "corporate memory" on relationship management but also paves the way for the establishment and implementation of measures and actions for crisis management and opportunities forecast.

Moreover, the CBI software is a dynamic tool – or database. In addition to the massive amount of domestic and international economic-financial data, political information, etc., the software allows the entry of data from a number of sources, such as competition monitoring and analysis, as well as from the market, government agencies, the press, conversations through social networks, amongst others. Such data, depending on its nature, is entered by the company's or the outsourced consultancy's team members.

The various pieces of information acquired and selected shall be collectively analyzed so that meaning can be specified and value can be added. Thus, meetings must be scheduled so that all participants involved (the company's, as well as the outsourced consultancy's Intelligence Cells) may interact personally throughout the analysis of the information acquired.

The objective, as preached by the IEAc concept, is not to reach uncertainties, but to generate assumptions that may decrease the uncertainties, infer actions and show the roadmap to discussions, simulations and specific investigations. The outcome of this process will provide subsidies for decision-making. To sum up, information will be selected. The outsourced consultancy's expertise must not only help collect data but also facilitate collective analysis, by questioning data, premises and conclusions.

After the implementation step is completed, and once the operation phase has kicked in, the whole process shall undergo weekly reviews, so that actions can be measured and the next steps can be mapped. In order to do that, the process, in its entirety, should be reported to the company's CEO, and to its planning area, along with the actions' results and the strategic conclusions.

CHAPTER 7
PERSONNEL PREPARATION, CBI'S GREAT CHALLENGE

> *"I hated every minute of training, but I said to myself: 'Do not give up. Suffer now and be a champion for the rest of your life'."*
>
> MUHAMMAD ALI

People comprise the underpinnings of the CBI Method Intelligence Cells. Technology is the support that provides more nimbleness in the job of data mining, analyzing, interacting, reaching conclusions, and transmitting these conclusions to the stakeholders. But people are what really matters!

The ideal, in a society in which information goes around with so much intensity and speed, would be to prepare the whole company's team for the acquisition of data and weak signals in the business environment, working in close cooperation with the outsourced consultancy's specialized team.

At the present juncture, going through in-company training processes is a fairly widespread practice, and this is not only due to the technological advances that demand an update. Training is also a means to stimulate more interest, on the part of the workforce, in its work, helping prevent red tape, and is, naturally, a process that is open to useful suggestions for better efficiency.

Furthermore, one can say training helps cell members promote the method throughout the company. There is always resistance. That reminds us of the famous words by boxer Muhammad Ali, who hated training but pressed on in order to become a champion. The cell's team must develop perception and attention with regard to information that is relevant to strategic issues previously established.

In order to evaluate training effectiveness, some questions must be answered after the Intelligence Cells have been operating for a while:

- To what extent have training goals been reached?
- What is the trainees' success rate as they implement the actions planned?
- To what extent have Intelligence Cell members asked coordinators for support?

The coordinators will be in charge or establishing the *modus operandi*, the available tools, the meeting schedule and the relationship agenda for information acquisition. We'd like to point out that training is not something related to a given occasion or situation only. It should focus on all aspects of the way the company works, encompassing an analysis of the competition, as well as that of new government regulations, which have been seen frequently in Brazil. We would need between 12 and 16 hours' worth of training, depending on the maturity of the selected team as far as the information analysis is concerned.

In this ideal situation, each member of the organization, during his or her day-to-day activities, would function as a kind of radar directed towards the market, shedding light on the shadowy spots indicated by these signals, in an attempt to turn them into the anticipation of events. Each individual, in his or her area, would manage, in a proactive manner, his/her curiosity with regard to the changes in the external environment, sharing the collected data with his/her co-workers, always focusing on the business' competitiveness and sustainability as time goes by.

The interaction amongst all individuals would give rise to associations, the identification of changes or disruptions, which would enable one to anticipate opportunities and the prevention of crises of any kind. Such anticipation, in turn, would provide the directions for the strategies and the decision-making in a constantly changing business environment.

Nevertheless, at the current stage of evolution of the corporate culture, we know that this wish should remain as it is: a wish. After all, a complete departure from behavior patterns established through years or decades of operation within the corporate environment does not come easy or quick. Amongst them one could mention corporatism, inter-department competition, the idea that "information is power" and even personal traits such as vanity, shyness and insecurity to face new things and face new challenges.

Who hasn't met, in a company, that extremely competent professional in his specialty, who is terrified of talking with more than one person at a time? Who hasn't been surprised, during a top management meeting, with a piece of information that, due to its impact on the business, should have been shared with everyone in management?

What raises flags is the fact that the main challenge refer, exactly to people – whether they are cell members, data miners or managers in charge of implementing the project. After all, one of the first challenges with regard to the cell establishment is that one must choose members who have certain personal traits, such as specific skills sets. And there are challenges with regard to the development of the work, to the skill-building, to the encouragement, so that everyone gets involved, to the process' management and organization, to the zeal for the quality of each team member's relationship within the cell and with the rest of the organization's team. Finally, there is another challenge: one must make sure the cell is known and respected by his/her peers throughout the organization.

The next few items in this chapter deal with the challenges associated with people. Most of these have already been indicated in the list of critical factors put together by Professor Janissek-Muniz. To facilitate understanding, they shall be divided according to the position that the professionals have with regard to the cell: manager in charge, coordinator and team in charge of acquiring information.

Before that, however, it is important to bear in mind that, when one chooses to establish Intelligence Cells, according to our CBI method, some of these factors tend to be mitigated. This is because one of the CBI features is that it makes senior professionals specialized in corporate management and public relations available to the project. These skills sets ensures they are able not only to make sure the work runs smoothly within the cell, but are also able to give managers and other professionals involved a heads-up on possible blind spots that may come up and that may be powerful enough to jeopardize the expected results.

CBI is a non-operational, strategic support project. In addition, it works across the board within the organization. Therefore, in order for it to meet its goals, in principle and in actual fact, the individual in charge of its establishment must have effective power. He or she must have a management position, preferably the president's seat. After all, if, one the one side, the president has the maximum power within the organization, on the other side, he or she is the individual who is most interested in the CBI's success, and he/she is also the end user of the work developed by the CBI.

As the end user of the information, only the president can have an overview of the business, detecting the corporate strategy's strengths and challenges, as well as those of every one of the areas involved. He or she, too, is the individual who will have access to the environments where the most "sophisticated" comments will be heard (that are not yet a matter of public record) with regard to the economy's evolution, politics, new management trends, and after all, business. And, finally, he or she is in charge of decision-making: his or her name – and nobody else's, will be revered due to the right moves and criticized due to the mistakes and omissions.

Therefore, even though he or she may be exposed to a flood of information, much of it totally irrelevant, the president knows – or at least he or she senses – where monitoring and analysis of signals that are able to serve as basis for decision-making, are the most critical for the whole organization's sustainability. A sales director or an operations' vice-president, even if we consider the point of view of his or her skills set and actuation, would naturally tend to direct the action of the IEAcs towards issues that are closer to their relevant areas.

In the period between 2003 and 2007, a multinational company, which operates in the electrical power sector in Brazil, worked according to a strategy which had, as one of its main goals, the recovery of its reputation, which had been slipping due to a number of factors, with regard to all of its stakeholders. Even though it did not have problems with the competition – utilities' concessions are nationwide monopolies – this reputation wear and tear was making it difficult for it to operate in all other areas: from hiring to the relationship with government agencies and domestic minor shareholders (seriously lacking in motivation) and customers.

In this process, three areas were considered strategic and of an across-the-board importance: regulatory affairs, human relations and communication/social accountability. All three of them, which traditionally had directorship status and reported to a vice-president, were turned into vice-president's offices – and, therefore, the president's direct reports. In addition, they all had access to management meetings, in which they could take the floor, but could not vote. Due to the changes, the professionals in charge of these areas could now have access to management-level decision-making; more interaction with the other areas; interaction with all hierarchical levels within the group.

The question that results from this example is: if the acquisition of market signals and the work of turning such signals into information are considered of strategic value by the organization, shouldn't the professionals in charge have a status that is compatible with the area's importance? Shouldn't they hold a position that would facilitate access to decision-making, to interaction with the other areas and to across-the-board action?

Now, evaluating the president as the individual who holds the maximum power within the organization: the CBI system, since it is new and innovative, will certainly meet some opposition on the part of the most conservative staff, who will feel threatened by the initiative towards democratizing information. The president has enough power to mitigate such opposition. A manager does not.

Imagine, for instance, how hard it would be for a marketing manager to convince the operations vice-president to release information that he considers strategic – even if it is not – about the competition. Or to spare a few minutes to meet with an Intelligence Cell member who is looking for some data that would complement a signal acquired. Or, even, who would admit that he has problems and needs help from the company's Intelligence with regard to a given project. Or, finally, that he would agree that a small competitor's ad, published in the employment section of daily newspapers, could signal strategic changes in the market that would put a whole production line of his company at risk.

For the president, or somebody at the same hierarchical level, it would be much easier to obtain results through initiatives like these. All it would take would be a WhatsApp massage, a phone call, or at the most, the addition of a subject in a management meeting.

For these reasons, in addition to power, the coordinator must have specific personal and professional characteristics, amongst which the interest for innovative processes and the capability to articulate and convince; planning; fund-raising for the project and the identification of weaknesses and blind spots within the company. Is there anyone better than the president or CEO to fit this description?

Some critical factors with regard to the manager*
Lack of support and get-up-and-go as required to start the intelligence project
Improper engagement on the part of management
Wrong establishment of expectations and goals desired with the intelligence project
No alignment between the project and the company's strategy
Hostile organizational culture
Budget too low
Underestimation of the project's complexity and its implications with regard to the organization

As listed by Professor Janissek-Muniz
* We'd like to point out that the individual referred to as the manager by the Professor, is the individual we call the coordinator, in the context of this book, as well as in the case of the CBI.

Leadership, the ability to motivate, in addition to an open mind regarding new knowledge acquisition and a sense of organization: these, to sum up, are the sine qua non characteristics for a CBI Intelligence Cell coordinator, whose final responsibility is to manage implementation and ensure the method is maintained as time goes by. This professional is essential for the process' success, in connection with the outsourced consultancy's team member.

It is important to point out that, in general, the company's Intelligence Cell coordinator has no experience in the subject – as he had been performing specific tasks in-house before the CBI process was introduced in the organization. Nevertheless, as opposed to the manager-creator – who sees the project in a strategic manner and in broad strokes – he will be one of the people that are responsible for its success.

Thus, the coordinator is like the captain who lifts the aircraft off the ground and keeps an eye on everything all the time in order to make sure the aircraft remains flying. But, as opposed to handling controls and machinery, the procedures involve people's management an articulation.

Therefore, on one side, the coordinator is responsible for, initially, choosing, and then, for motivating, organizing and managing the group's team members and projects. He has to prove, in practice and for the whole organization, the importance of the work done – which involves, in addition to the presentation of concrete results, the inter-personal relationships.

Between one thing and the other – and due to both – there is, in addition, the responsibility to establish focus and to teach the information user the question that must be asked in order to get the right answer. Therefore, it is understandable that Professor Janissek-Muniz specifies, as the two sine qua non skills for the coordinator, the ability to motivate and to manage. These skills may be acquired as long as the professional has the role of the animator as his/her own personal trait. With regard to the role of the animator, she points out: "The ability to motivate an IEAc device is a required skill, so that it may run smoothly and continuously as time goes by" (article: "Identifying skills to motivate Anticipative and Collective Strategy: Proposing the tool to oversee the development of new motivators").

To sum up, if one is to validate the cells within the organization, from square one, one shall depend on person-to-person interactions so that the fundamental doubt will appear, which, in turn, will elicit the proper response. This is what we call a target. And on this subject, Janissek-Muniz quotes Boulifa-Tamboura (2008): "If it is too narrow, it will not address the decision-makers' concerns. If it is too broad, it presents too much information and nothing that really matters. If the limitations and priorities are not properly established, there is a risk of an information overload, or lack of it, as well as discouragement and an impact on the way in which the remaining steps of the device are implemented".

Some critical factors associated with the coordinator*
Lack of appropriate skills
Failure to plan the project
Errors while identifying the requirements, and thus, in collecting information
Improper management
Believing in solutions that are of a technical nature only for problems that are, essentially, managerial in nature.
Underestimating the project's complexity and its implications within the organization
Improper use of analysis tools and techniques
Poor communication and poor promotion of intelligence products

As listed by Professor Janissek-Muniz

Examples of requests or demands that may result in failure in the coordinator's job are mentioned in the book *Inteligência Estratégica Antecipativa e Coletiva: O Método L.E.SCAnning*, [Strategic, Anticipative and Collective Intelligence: The L.E.SCAnning] written by Humbert Lesca and Professor Janissek-Muniz.

Team members: the pyramid's basis and its greatest challenge

Data collection is a subtle job. It demands organization effort, will and motivation. The data miner is the individual who has initial contact with the information. He or she is the one who shall decide whether to reject the information or to disclose it to the group. Here we may deal with three situations, according to Professor Janissek-Muniz:

- The data miner sends a piece of information of no great interest. This is not a very serious situation, even though it may result in an overload of variables and may contribute to provide the users with more information than they can handle;
- The data miner mistakenly rejects a piece of information. Nobody is made aware of this fact. This is a more serious situation, especially if the information is of any value to the user;
- The data miner sends a piece of information of great value to the potential user. This is the ideal situation.

The data miner's profile and skills set, therefore, are of the utmost importance for the cells' success. This professional's attitude will always have an impact on the development of the work – for better or worse. The screening of the colletors will probably be the largest challenge in the establishment of the cells.

Remember that these professionals are selected within various departments and they must add data mining and gathering to their other day-to-day duties. And finally, remember that, at the present juncture, these duties are no mean feat. If, until a few years back, people would resent not having money, now they complain, mainly, about not having enough time. A poll performed in November 2013 by Instituto Brasileiro de Opinião Pública e Estatística (Ibope), encompassing about 1,500 internet users, revealed the fact that 98% of them consider their day-to-day rush and the stress resulting there from as the main reasons why they feel tired.

Finally, it is important to point out that it is in this group that the differences in personalities and skills sets are most visible. If team members are not carefully picked, this is where shy and insecure professionals will be found. These people are afraid of new things and of the collective exposure to new ideals.

Therefore, until such time as the information culture has been consolidated within the organization and the will to acquire data is evaluated as a natural attitude, one must consider that the professionals who are members of the IEAc cells may see this process as an extra activity, in their day-to-day activities that are already quite intense. "In this sense Martinet and Ribault (1989) noticed that participants were motivated early in the process but, they tend to lose interest quite rapidly, that is, once the initial excitement due to the device's implementation is gone, a certain amount of exhaustion is perceived across the board", records Professor Janissek-Muniz.

This context of discouragement and a perception of activities in excess may lead to situations that might jeopardize success. Amongst them we can mention conflict amongst team members, lack (individually or collectively) of commitment or even the fact that some team members involved with the CBI system, based on IEAcs, may have been transferred to another department or may have left the company.

Some critical factors with regard to team members *
Lack of knowledge to start data gathering activities
Improper skills set and lack of training
The lack of qualified agents to monitor this work
Lack of motivation and reward
Not enough time is allocated to monitoring
Lack of confidence and cooperation amongst team members
People's tendency to prefer to ignore a warning so as not to disturb the group's consensus

* Prof. Janissek-Muniz

The professor also points out that the coordinator's position, as of the moment in which the data miners are selected, is vital in order to work one's way around these problems, or mitigate them. Summarizing, amongst the steps required so that this team's work can run smoothly, we could stress the following:

- The team's preparation and sensitivity training;
- The need for the data miners to have a fairly high knowledge level;
- Encourage the people who are in touch with the external environment to be aware of and collect/transmit information;

- Help data miners occasionally, by means of specific advice and small bits of information for specific purposes;
- Continuous encouragement;
- Encourage data miners to work voluntarily;
- Foster a spirit due to which data miners will enjoy spending time together, being partners and will interact with one another;
- Encourage feedback with regard to the use of selected information;
- Make sure the organization sees the network of data miners and their role in the process;
- The need to make the information selection process formal.

Considering that the relationship above, as a whole, is the responsibility of one professional – the coordinator – one can conclude that his position is vital so that the work runs smoothly and so that satisfactory results can be achieved. If we add, to such responsibility, all the difficulties inherent to the consolidation and validation of IEAcs with regard to the other areas, one can see why this coordinator requires support from the organization's management in order to succeed in his work.

CLOSING REMARKS

AND WHEN YOUR DOG WAGS HIS TAIL....

Intelligence misleads us to a secret operation. Maybe this is why, when I introduced this concept to the CEO of a large corporation, the visit felt markedly uncomfortable. After I assured him I was not carrying a tape recorder, and that my pen was not a video camera, he smiled and made himself a little more at ease, in spite of the fact that once in a while he would shoot a glance towards my eyeglasses in the vain hope that he could find evidence that somebody else had eyes on him.

To tell the truth, this scene mentioned above did not happen exactly as I described it. I was only being creative in order to make up for my frustration for not being engaged in writing a work of fiction. I decided to put my imagination on the driver's seat, to some extent. Actually, when I seek to demonstrate CBI, I sense a touch of concern about what I will, in fact, be dealing with.

But during one of many presentations, after I explained the underpinnings of the process, an executive expressed his concern about the fact that strategic data would be recorded by means of a software product that would be shared amongst "the rank and file" in his company's payroll (this is what he said), exposing a number of things, such as secrets, government relations, deals and schemes, influences, lobbies, weaknesses and, possibly, even compliance-related vulnerabilities.

I believe I made it quite clear, on previous pages hereof, that we are not making a case for the establishment of an MI5 unit embedded with your company. By the same token, we are not suggesting that the cell's members spy or engage in behavior other than that related to data retrieval, recording and analysis. I am thoroughly convinced that you have been surprised, several times, upon becoming aware that the "rank and file" – as described - has come up with a relevant information or piece of information in the course of a discussion about a given issue. Yes, you are bound to be taken by surprise when the cells start connecting the dots.

I look at my hand even as I type these words. It has a small scar. Two weeks ago, as I was on my farm, my dog jumped on me and his paw made a deep cut. Now I picture the work of the intelligent cells, as Professor Lipton would put it, as they tried to piece together this small incident. Can you imagine how many pieces of information were transmitted to my brain in thousandths of a second?

How such information was processed so as to stanch the bleeding, identify harmful invaders and set the defenses in motion, in addition to initiating the healing process? As of now, your company is exposed to outside threats every thousandth of a second, and you know that, better than anyone else. Threats do not came at you *wagging* their tails, like a dog who has missed its owner, and is reunited with him. Threats can be disguised as in innovation. They can be created by a regulatory agency, they can come up during a discussion in Congress, or maybe in an employee's attitude with regard to a consumer.

Vulnerabilities may be perceived and anticipated if you pay attention to the weak signals that may be in the room next door. Make sure the information flows within your company and everyone is made aware of the issues, as well as the risks that are a cause of concern to you. Provide the cells with the required means and the nimbleness, so they can let the brain know what is going on. Information should no longer be treated as a secret that only a few are privy to, under lock and key, in a room filled with codes and secrets. Not even your codes in your systems are safe. The flow of information is safe because, with it, you will listen to the weak signals and will follow them as far as the point of change – the moment at which they will call for the pre-emptive decision-making that will set you apart from the competitors and will ensure you are ready for what lies ahead.

How often have you surprised yourself stating repeatedly that the world has changed? How often have you said that you cannot keep up with the quick pace of technology and the sheer volume of information that you receive on a daily basis? Aren't you tired of hearing experts saying the same thing in seminars that you attend?

Anyway, what do you actually do in order to be able to keep abreast of these changes? Instead of showing that you are well aware of the changes, wouldn't you rather understand that you too must change? Wouldn't the changes, the quick pace at which the information flows, trigger a retooling, by you, and by your organization, so that you would be able to live according to this new status quo?

The question is: what have you or your organization done in order to deal with this brutal volume of information that you receive every day? Doesn't the revolution also demand changes in the way you deal with it? Recognizing the change is not enough. Become part of it. The sheer fear of becoming obsolete is not enough. Face the music. Push the envelope. Is your organization flashing by just like the information? How does data flow within your company? What decisions have you made in order to ensure it flows in-house as quickly as it comes in?

According to the March 16, 2017 issue of newspaper *Valor Econômico*, almost every day we become aware of cyber-attacks. "About 50 million attempts are made every year. Brazil is the third country in the number of attacks it is the target of, after the United Stated and China. Only in Brazil, 100 thousand attacks take place every day. The global cost of cyber-attacks is estimated to be in the order of US$ 600 Billion per year. This amount is nearly the same as that associated with the illicit drug trade."

According to the experts, and also according to the *Valor Econômico* newspaper "the underworld of the worldwide computer network, known as the Dark web, corresponds to 6% of all information made available through the worldwide computer network, whereas the search engines, including Google, represent 4%. The remaining 90% is stored in databases held by governments, academic institutions, medical organizations, etc."

I believe we have before us, more than just answers. We have actual examples of perfection and balance: in the Universe, in nature and in the human body. By observing only these three examples, shouldn't we be able to learn something from them? As I usually say, the analogy between the inner workings of the human body and the way many things operate, including companies, the corporate environment, the *esprit de corps*, corporatism, was not created yesterday...

Wise man says that when we seek answers we can find them by "looking into ourselves". Have you looked into your company? Maybe the more you look the more answers you will find. Look into yourself and you will find a regular man seeking answers with regard to your own professional restlessness.

And when your dog comes, affectively wagging his tail, you will be able to prevent scrapes and bruises to your hand.

If you can, pat your dog and sit on the lawn with it. Gather your loved ones, your family members, around you. Just listen to what the others are saying. You will appreciate the conversation, and during information exchange that takes place about day-to-day things, at home, at the club, you may be surprised to see so much information that can be processed.

It looks too simple.

But it works.

ACKNOWLEDGEMENTS

Actually, the proper title above should be merits instead of acknowledgements, since merit is something one does which deserves compliments and recognition. In the specific case of this work, merit should be shared with Professor Raquel Janissek-Muniz, Vitor Madeira, Claudia Mancini and Béatrice Seguin, in addition to, of course, Professor Humbert Lesca and the team from Pierre Mendès-France University, Grenoble, France, who have been working on the study of the Anticipative Intelligence method for over 30 years.

It took us many years of discussion, during almost one year, before we were able to complete the content as well as the rationale of this method, CBI, which we could say, only complements the brilliant work of the Grenoble scientists. The inclusion of this model for the communication agencies as the main outsourced complementary agents of this corporate culture change, can, and should be considered an effective contribution.

My friend, journalist Klaus Kleber, put together the first draft of our ideals, and provided the format of what this book would become. His contribution was vital and it was a motivation so that we could go on. Throughout this period Mr. Kleber had to hold a number of meetings, and engage in debates, adjustments and research work. If he could, he would have gone to Waterloo, to ask Napoleon whether he had any contact with the Rothschild family.

A word of thanks to the CEOs who were generous with their time to share with me, in an open and clear-cut manner, their concerns and confidences, especially Gustavo Valle, who, from Paris, has been encouraging me a great deal, and in Brazil, to journalists Paulo Nassar, Antonio Costa Filho, Eurípedes Alcântara and Fernanda Nóbrega.

And, last but not least, without my Editor Eliana Sá's enthusiasm and competence, none of this would have been possible. She was the one who let me know how difficult it is to write a book. With her permanent smile, her eyes full of energy and her peculiar manner, Mrs. Sá was able to put the ideas in order and to get, out of me, a little gentleness in the way of expressing these concepts and thoughts.

CBI TEAM

Raquel Janissek-Muniz
Graduated in Informatics with emphasis in Systems Analysis (UNIJUÍ-RS, 1995), Master in Management by the School of Management (Universidade Federal do Rio Grande do Sul (UFRGS), 2000), Master DEA MATIS (University of Geneva, Switzerland, 2001), Master DEA in Systèmes d'Information (Université Pierre Mendès-France, 2001), Ph.D. in Management Sciences (Université Pierre Mendès-France, 2004) and Post-Doctorate in Management (GIANTI-PPGA, EA, UFRGS, 2005-2006).

Since 2006, she is an Associate Professor at the School of Management (PPGA/EA/UFRGS). She is active in the following disciplines: Organizational Systemic View, Intelligence and Knowledge, Theories and Methods in Information Systems, Process and Method in Strategic Intelligence and Research Workshop on Information Systems.

Key research and top interests: Strategic and anticipative intelligence, Weak Signals, Environmental Scanning, Methods and

Practices in Environmental Scanning and Knowledge Management.

Coordinator IITI Group (http://www.ufrgs.br/grupo-iiti), IEA Brasil Coordinator (http://www.ieabrasil.com.br), Coordinator Strategic Intelligence Specialization Program at UFRGS School of Business Administration, and Coordinator GSTI (Systems Management and Information Technology) at UFRGS PPGA (Business Management Post-Graduate Program).

Claudia Mancini

Graduated in Journalism at Pontifical Catholic University of São Paulo (PUC-SP) and has a Master's in Latin American Studies from the University of London (Institute of Latin American Studies/ London School of Economics), as well as a Master's degree in Political Science from University of São Paulo (USP).Claudia started her career as a journalist at *Gazeta Mercantil*, where she occupied successive positions from reporter to editor in chief in a period of 18 years. She also worked as a reporter at Dow Jones Newswires in London. In 2008, she became a Communications consultant at agency CDN, working exclusively for the Brazilian Federation of Banks. In 2010, she joined MSLGROUP-Andreoli to manage the business unit focused on the financial and aerospace sectors and on international institutions and foreign governments. Later, she was part of the team who set up MSLGROUP Publicis Consultants, a unit focused on communications based on strategic intelligence and focused on complex issues. At this unit, she implemented the Cellular Business Intelligence method.

Vitor Madeira
Vice-President, heading IBM's Financial Services Practice in Latin America, responsible for strategy and organization projects. He has more than 25 years of experience in consulting to Financial Institutions.
Before joining IBM, he was Vice-President of Arthur D. Little, a member of its Latin American board and responsible for its Financial Industries Practice in Latin America. He was also President of A. T. Kearney in Brazil and also responsible for its Financial Industries Practice in Latin America.
He was the leader of several relevant projects in Strategy and Organization for the main regional Financial Institutions. Before entering in consulting, he was an executive in companies at the Media industry and also at a major Scientific Research Institution.
He graduated in Industrial Engineering at the Polytechnic School at the University of São Paulo.

Béatrice Seguin

Undergraduate Degree in Economics and Political Science from the Political Science School (Science-Po), Paris, France; Master's Degree in Economics and Politics, from the University of Hamburg; currently finishing Business Management graduate studies at Dom Cabral Foundation. For the last 12 years she has been active in projects engaged in the promotion of the European Union in Germany, in the European Parliament in Belgium, at Publicis Consultants in France and in Brazil. She has nine years' experience in corporate communications, both in the public and in the private sector. She has been engaged in strategic communication work for large corporations such as Danone, AXA, Accor Hotels, GRU Airport, GDF Suez, Coca Cola, Carlyle Institute, *The Economist*, the Mexican government and French institutions such as Sécurité Routière (Highway Security Agency) Agence Française pour le Développement (French Development Agency), L'Autorité de régulation des jeux en ligne (Online Games Regulatory Agency) among others. Alongside with the MSLGROUP Brazil team, Béatrice was engaged in developing solutions for the Cellular Business Intelligence. At the present juncture she works as a communication *freelancer* and also as the Communication Director at Engaja Brasil, a social enterprise established in order to help NGOs diversify their funding sources.

ABOUT THE AUTHOR

Paulo Andreoli
Chairman do MSL Latin America,
CEO e presidente da MSL Andreoli

64 years old, has substantial experience as a journalist, executive and businessman. He has been for two consecutive years considered one of the most influential professionals in the PR industry in the world by the prestigious publication PRWeek. In 1994, after leaving the Corporate Affairs Board at the O *Estado de S. Paulo* Group, he founded Paulo Andreoli & Associados, a pioneering Corporate Affairs agency in Brazil, currently known as Andreoli/MS&L, one of the largest agencies in Brazil today which stands out on the market for its strategic approach to corporate issues. Andreoli/MS&L is part of the Publicis Groupe global Public Relations network. Graduating in Sociology from the Politics and Sociology School at the University of Sao Paulo, he took university extension and specialization courses in Nuclear Physics at the Physics Institute (USP), International Law (focusing on

Nuclear Law) at the Law Faculty (USP) and in international trade, at the Konrad Adenauer Foundation in Bonn, Germany. As a journalist he always worked at O *Estado de São Paulo*. In 1979, he received the Esso award – considered the Latin American version of the Pulitzer Prize. As a director of the newspaper O Estado de São Paulo Group, he was involved in the NNA – National Newspaper Association – which represents Brazilian newspapers owners. He was a member of the IPS – Inter-American Press Society – and organized the 47th Annual Assembly in Sao Paulo, in 1991. Between 1982 and 1989 he was president of Zanini International Trading Co. and shareholder and CEO in Wolf International Trading Co. He is a member of the board at Carlyle Institute, was a member at Fernand Braudel World Economy Institute and was country chairman for the International Public Relations Association in Brazil.

BIBLIOGRAPHIC REFERENCES

ANSOFF, I. H. "Managing strategic surprise by response to weak signals". *California Management Review Winter*. 75, v. 18, n. 2, p. 21-33, 1975.

JANISSEK-MUNIZ, R. "Fatores críticos em projetos de Inteligência Estratégica Antecipativa e Coletiva". *Revista Inteligência Competitiva*. v. 6, n. 2, p. 147-180, 2016.

JANISSEK-MUNIZ, R.; LESCA, H.; FREITAS, H. "Inteligência Estratégica Antecipativa e Coletiva para tomada de decisão". Revista *Organizações em Contexto*: Universidade Metodista de São Paulo. Ano II. n. 4. Dez. 2006.

LESCA, H.; JANISSEK-MUNIZ, R. *Inteligência Estratégica Antecipativa e Coletiva: o Método L.E.SCAnning*. Porto Alegre.188 p.

LIPTON, H. BRUCE.*The biology of belief: Unleashing the power of consciousness, matter and miracles*. California: Hay House. 2005. 314 p.

This work was composed in S<small>ABON</small> and D<small>AX</small>
by G<small>RAPHIC</small> D<small>ESIGN</small> and printed on offset by
B<small>ARTIRA</small> G<small>RÁFICA E</small> E<small>DITORA</small> L<small>TDA</small>. on C<small>HAMBRIL</small> A<small>VENA</small> LD soft 90g paper
of Suzano Papel e Celulose for Paulo Andreoli Editor,
in September 2017